Denise Burkhard

Ancient Dwarf Kingdom or the Hoard of a Fiery Dragon?

Denise Burkhard

Ancient Dwarf Kingdom or the Hoard of a Fiery Dragon?

J. R. R. Tolkien's Erebor as a Transformed and Dynamic Place

Tectum Verlag

Denise Burkhard
Ancient Dwarf Kingdom or the Hoard of a Fiery Dragon?
J. R. R. Tolkien's Erebor as a Transformed and Dynamic Place

ISBN 978-3-8288-3975-5
eISBN 978-3-8288-6774-1

Umschlaggestaltung: Tectum Verlag, unter Verwendung des Bildes # 279005717
von Bon Appetit | www.shutterstock.com

Printed in Germany

Besuchen Sie uns im Internet
www.tectum-verlag.de

Bibliografische Informationen der Deutschen Nationalbibliothek
Die Deutsche Nationalbibliothek verzeichnet diese Publikation
in der Deutschen Nationalbibliografie; detaillierte bibliografische
Angaben sind im Internet über http://dnb.ddb.de abrufbar.

Contents

Acknowledgements

I would like to express my gratitude to a number of people, who supported me with their helpful advice in various ways.

First and foremost, I am grateful to my supervisor Prof. Dr. Marion Gymnich, who provided me with invaluable support, kind guidance and constructive feedback whenever it was needed, and encouraged me to publish this bachelor thesis. Special thanks also to my second supervisor Dr. Hanne Birk for her highly useful suggestions, her encouragement and her friendly advice. Moreover, I would like to thank Benjamin Schnaidt for proofreading this book. I am very grateful for his extremely thorough and helpful comments on matters of language and content, specifically on "Part I: Approaching the Spatial Dimension". Finally, I wish to thank three of my fellow students for their support and valuable feedback.

Introduction:
Or "'I am looking for someone to share in an adventure'"[1]

In J.R.R. Tolkien's children's novel *The Hobbit, or There and Back Again* (1937), Erebor[2] is not only a place on a map marked by a red dragon and a dwarvish rune but a mountain in which the ancient and majestic dwarf kingdom had been built. Before the dragon attacked the mountain, the treasures of Erebor had been legendary and the kingdom within the mountain had grown wealthy and prosperous. Its halls had been "'full of armour and jewels and carvings and cups'"[3], fashioned from metals and gemstones the dwarves[4] found in the depths of the mountain. But "the rumour of the wealth of Erebor spread abroad and reached the ears of the dragons"[5], and the fierce and sinister Smaug was attracted by the golden treasure. When he came down from the North, he conquered the dwarf kingdom, dispersed the mountain's inhabitants and converted the treasure into "a bed of gold"[6]. Although Erebor has been occupied by the dragon since that day, its former inhabitants still remember their erstwhile kingdom and attempt to reclaim the mountain.

Against this background, Erebor is not only one of the most significant and virtually ever-present places in the story, but at the same time one of its most ambivalent ones, which has up until now not received extensive scholarly attention.[7] Throughout this book, I will read Erebor as a multiply encoded place and

---

1 J.R.R. Tolkien. *The Hobbit*, 7.

2 'Erebor' is the Sindarin (Elvish) word for the 'Lonely Mountain'; the two terms will be used synonymously.

3 J.R.R. Tolkien. *The Hobbit*, 28.

4 Tolkien explained his idiosyncratic spelling of the plural of 'dwarf' in a letter to the editor of the 'Observer': "Grammar prescribes *dwarfs*; philology suggests that *dwarrows* would be the historical form. The real answer is that I knew no better. But *dwarves* goes well with *elves*; and, in any case, *elf*, *gnome*, *goblin*, *dwarf* are only approximate translations of the Old Elvish names for beings of not quite the same kinds and functions". Humphrey Carpenter (Ed.). *Letters of J.R.R. Tolkien*, 31 [Letter 25: To the editor of the 'Observer', February 1938], original emphasis. I will, thus, adopt Tolkien's spelling and his use of small letters in the names for the peoples of Middle-earth, which some scholars tend to capitalise.

5 J.R.R. Tolkien. *The Return of the King*, 1408.

6 Ibid.

7 Jane Suzanne Carroll also stresses the fact that in contrast to scholars' keen interest in language in Tolkien's writings "there is comparatively little critical interest in the role of landscape in his fiction", and encourages the analysis of the depiction of landscape by observing that "Tolkien was acutely aware of the significance of topography, and the wealth of landscape detail within his fiction and the rich cartography surrounding it lend weight to this awareness". Jane Suzanne Carroll. "A Topoanalytical Reading of Landscapes.", 122-23.

focus on its ambivalent representation as an ancient dwarf kingdom, which comes to life in the dwarves' memories, and as a dragon's hoard, which is guarded by Smaug the Golden. Hence my focus will be on the introduction, destruction and reconstruction of Erebor, and further on the extent to which these facets contribute to the perception of the mountain as a transformed and dynamic place.

In my analysis, I assume that "the fantasy 'other' world structures and maintains *a* reality"[8]. This assumption is supported by Tolkien himself, who put forward in his lecture "On Fairy Stories"[9] that the secondary world, 'Faërie', "contains many things besides elves and fays, and besides dwarfs, witches, trolls, giants, or dragons: it holds the seas, the sun, the moon, the sky; and the earth, and all things that are in it"[10]. On this basis, I suppose that such other worlds are self-contained and autonomous worlds that consist of several distinct places and spaces, which can be explored by the characters of the story. With respect to Tolkien's writings, Liam Campbell notices a striking emphasis on natural environments:

> [w]hen visiting the writings of Tolkien, one is immediately struck by the sheer multiplicity of represented, reconceived, and imagined natural elements [...]: there are highly detailed and vibrant passages that focus on not only trees, flora, grasslands, and waterways, but also weather, phases of the moon, wilderness, unforgiving mountains, swamps, and passing seasons.[11]

All of these highlight the relevance of topography and its complexity in Tolkien's world and suggest that an analysis of the Lonely Mountain will be rewarding. The aim of 'Part I: Approaching the Spatial Dimension' is to provide a theoretical basis on which Erebor can be analysed as a place and as a home. It will focus on aspects and characteristics associated with places and spaces in literature, such as movement and perception, and will elaborate on the notion of 'home' in children's literature. This discussion will be based on the "intimately intertwined"[12] concepts (narrative) place and (narrative) space.

In the following subchapter, I will look more closely at the term 'diaspora' in postcolonial approaches. While the term "is traditionally used with reference to Jewish history where it describes the experience, predominant at least since the destruction of the temple in Jerusalem in 133 A.D., of living outside the Holy Land"[13], it is also used to describe the forceful movement of peoples and "can

---

8 Anthony Pavlik. *A View from Elsewhere*, 20, original emphasis.

9 This lecture was held in the context of the Andrew Lang Lecture series in 1938, one year after *The Hobbit* was published. However, it was not published as an essay before 1947.

10 J.R.R. Tolkien. "Tree and Leaf.", 38.

11 Liam Campbell. "Nature.", 431.

12 Nicole Schröder. *Spaces and Places in Motion*, 45., see also: J.E. Malpas. *Place and Experience*, 19.

13 Tobias Döring. *Postcolonial Literatures in English*, 30.

refer to ‘any body of people living outside of their homeland’”[14]. In his letter to Naomi Mitchison, Tolkien alludes to Jewish history when he explains: “I do think of the ‘Dwarves’ like Jews: at once native and alien in their habitations, speaking the languages of the country, but with an accent due to their own private tongue”[15]. Tolkien’s statement suggests that Thorin Oakenshield and his company are caught in a ‘diasporic state’ out of which they reconstruct their kingdom. This ‘diasporic state’ has several implications for the people, such as a (re-)negotiation of the sense of home and the sense of belonging which may even gain (new) meanings.[16] In this context, the strong connection between memory, nostalgia and home will be highlighted,[17] since they feature prominently in Tolkien’s *The Hobbit.*

‘Part II: The Dwarf Kingdom’ and ‘Part III: The Dragon’s Hoard’ will focus on the depiction of Erebor in Tolkien’s *The Hobbit* and in Peter Jackson’s adaptations of the novel: *The Hobbit – An Unexpected Journey* (2012), *The Hobbit – The Desolation of Smaug* (2013) and *The Hobbit – The Battle of the Five Armies* (2014).[18] At the outset of Part II, the dwarves will be introduced by examining their origins in Tolkien’s world in the chapter “A Brief Introduction to the Depiction of Dwarves in Tolkien’s Writings”. This chapter will be followed by an analysis of the dwarves’ diasporic situation. I will focus on their history and the specific choice of words used in references to Erebor, which reflect the situation of the dwarves at the beginning of the story.[19] Homeless, restless and determined to regain Erebor, their collective memory gives Bilbo and the reader an introduction to and a retrospective glimpse at their former kingdom in the first part of the ‘Song of the Lonely Mountain’. This song is the first – even if only imaginary – encounter for both the reader and the protagonist Bilbo Baggins with the Lonely Mountain and the dwarf kingdom of old. Corey Olsen highlights the song’s importance in terms of characterisation by stating that it is “[t]he best

14 Justin D. Edwards. *Postcolonial Literature*, 150. Edwards quotes from the 1993 edition of the *Shorter Oxford Dictionary.*

15 Humphrey Carpenter. *Letters of J.R.R. Tolkien*, 229 [Letter 176: From a letter to Naomi Mitchison, 8 December 1955].

16 Cf. John McLeod. *Beginning Postcolonialism*, 248.

17 Dennis Walder emphasises the connection between memory and nostalgia in a postcolonial context and suggests that they are almost inseparable: “It is of course possible to recall and reflect upon the past as an individual or a group without being affected by nostalgia, although it is often difficult to disentangle nostalgic feelings from the operations of memory more generally”. Dennis Walder. *Postcolonial Nostalgias*, 4.

18 This comparative approach seems to be particularly promising, because “[t]he setting of *The Hobbit* represents a clear challenge to the film maker. Description is sparse”. Frank P. Riga, Maureen Thum and Judith Kollmann. “From Children’s Book to Epic Prequel.”, 104.

19 In this context, it is crucial to acknowledge that “[t]he narrative may not be written from a dwarvish point of view, but it allows the reader a glimpse of dwarven society from the inside”, which makes it possible to assess the dwarves’ situation at the beginning of the story. Gerard Hynes. “From Nauglath to Durin’s Folk.”, 25.

introduction that we get to the dwarves"[20], which is the reason why I will pay special attention to this song. Moreover, the dwarves' treasure will be closely examined. This treasure consists not only of gold and silver, but, as indicated before, of precious gems, filigree objects as well as weapons and armour and contains the most precious and valuable piece of the whole hoard, the Arkenstone of Thrain. I will argue for a body metaphor that can be found in Jackson's adaptations as well as in the stone's alternative name "Heart of the Mountain"[21]. In this context, I will also analyse the visual creation of Erebor in Jackson's *An Unexpected Journey*, which is roughly based on Tolkien's story and elaborates on the appearance of Erebor. It is not only that Jackson changed the sequence of scenes in comparison to the order of information provided in *The Hobbit*, but he also visually created places that have never been described, or which are not described in a detailed way. These comprise some of the exterior parts of the mountain, such as Dale, as well as interior parts, for instance Thror's throne room; Peter Jackson even 'built' an entire city within the Lonely Mountain that reinforces the sheer dimension of the dwarf kingdom and the vast number of its inhabitants.

'Part III: The Dragon's Hoard' will be concerned with the kingdom's destruction through the dwarves' fiery antagonist Smaug the Golden. First of all, I will have a closer look at dragons' characteristics in Tolkien's writings in the chapter "A Brief Introduction to Tolkien's Dragons". This introductory chapter will be followed by an analysis of the second part of the 'Song of the Lonely Mountain', which deals not only with the dragon's attack but also with issues that allow comparisons between Erebor's past and present state. Moreover, I will have a closer look at the first chapter for additional information that characterises Smaug. In this context, I will take his full name as well as his epithet 'the Golden' into account and argue that he is the vicious monster of the story – an aspect which is emphasised by his hybrid nature, which has been linked with his 'uncanny appearance'.[22] My third subchapter is not only concerned with comparisons between the former and present state of Erebor, it also stresses the use of Gothic elements and highlights the mountain's 'transformability'. Furthermore, I will address the strong link between the characters and the mountain and discuss in how far they are able to recreate the kingdom of old. Finally, I will examine the front gate, 'the Gallery of the Kings' and the treasure chamber in terms of their meaning, function and in the form of their reshaping or their destruction in both Tolkien's novel and Peter Jackson's *The Hobbit* trilogy.

20 Corey Olsen. *Exploring* The Hobbit, 29.

21 J.R.R. Tolkien. *The Hobbit*, 268.

22 Cf. Ármann Jakobsson. "Talk to the Dragon.", 27-28.; cf. Emily Midkiff. "Uncanny Dragons.", 47.

PART I:
APPROACHING THE SPATIAL DIMENSION

1.1 Place and Space in Literature

'Multilayered', 'complex' and 'entwined' may be the best words to describe the ambiguous nature of the terms 'place' and 'space'. Despite the fact that "[p]lace and its most frequent companion term, space, seem to be on everyone's lips in recent years, across multiple domains of academic discourse as well as popular culture"[23], they still need a clear definition. This lack of a precise definition can be assigned to multiple reasons; J.E. Malpas, for example, assumes that

> it is not just our everyday familiarity with the concept ['place'] that can give rise to difficulties, but also a complexity and breadth of meaning that seems to attach to the term itself. The English 'place' carries a variety of senses and stands in close relation to a number of terms that cover a very broad range of concepts.[24]

Moreover, "its transfer to more theoretical contexts is likely to present an immediate problem"[25] exactly because the term is so commonplace. A third problem is that spatial relations have largely been neglected for some time: Sabine Buchholz and Manfred Jahn argue "that space in narratives – especially pre-nineteenth-century ones – often seemed to have no other function than to supply a general background setting, something to be taken for granted rather than requiring attention, far less essential than the temporal directedness [...] of the plot"[26]. This helps to explain the comparative scarcity of spatial description in literary texts. In addition, H. Porter Abbott speculates "that the neglect of space in the study of narrative may have come from the fact that narrative scholars, especially in the early years, tended to focus on verbal narrative, oral and written"[27] and that it may have been the strong focus on suspense, which "is time-intensive"[28], that diverted attention from space.

In the second half of the twentieth century, an increasing interest in the concept of space has become known as the 'spatial turn'. This term was coined by the urban planner Edward William Soja, who claimed that a rethinking of the

---

23 Greg Dickinson et al. "Introduction: Rhetoric/Memory/Place.", 22.

24 J.E. Malpas. *Place and Experience*, 21. Gabriel Zoran makes a similar observation with regard to 'space' and claims that "[a]lthough the subject of space has been dealt with more than once, research in general on the subject is quite diffuse, and there are few assumptions that have become generally accepted". Gabriel Zoran. "Towards a Theory of Space in Narrative.", 310.

25 J.E. Malpas. *Place and Experience*, 21.

26 Sabine Buchholz and Manfred Jahn. "Space in Narrative.", 551. This is their second reason why the "consideration of space got off to a slow start"; they list "Gotthold Ephraim Lessing's characterisation of narrative literature as a 'temporal' art" as the first reason. Ibid.

27 H. Porter Abbott. *The Cambridge Introduction to Narrative*, 160.

28 Ibid.

existing notions of space in the social sciences and humanities was required.[29] The existing concepts were, for instance, based on the Euclidean/Cartesian concepts. They often "encompassed a belief in an absolute space and that material spaces could be truthfully, accurately and objectively represented"[30]. They were refined and new concepts were developed. This demand for and importance of a rethinking of the existing concepts was also highlighted by the French philosopher Michel Foucault. In his lecture on *Des Espaces Autres* ("Of Other Spaces") in 1967, he argued:

> The present epoch will perhaps be above all the epoch of space. We are in the epoch of simultaneity: we are in the epoch of juxtaposition, the epoch of the near and far, of the side-by-side, of the dispersed. We are at a moment, I believe, when our experience of the world is less that of a long life developing through time than that of a network that connects points and intersects with its own skein.[31]

He claimed not only that "concepts of locality and position"[32] played a major role in his perception of the world, but also that the focus had shifted from time towards spatial relations – towards the individual and his or her interactions with and within spaces and places.

Despite the fact that the notions 'place' and 'space' have gained scholarly attention by now, definitions are far from being unambiguous and the sheer variety of definitions of both terms means that there are diverse uses of the concepts. As J.E. Malpas argues with focus on 'place', "many of the discussions of place in the existing literature suggest that the notion is not at all clearly defined"[33]. Nicole Schröder is also aware of the multitude of definitions and points to the lack of consensus:

> Although there is no unanimous opinion with regard to the distinction between these two terms, it seems that – at least in everyday use – space appears to be the more general term; it implies a certain expansion and is therefore to a certain extent unknowable, whereas

---

29 Cf. Wolfgang Hallet and Birgit Neumann. "Raum und Bewegung in der Literatur.", 11-12.

30 Anthony Pavlik. *A View from Elsewhere*, 24.

31 Michel Foucault. "Of Other Spaces.", 22.

32 J.E. Malpas. *Place and Experience*, 20.

33 Ibid., 19. For example, Milford A. Jeremiah lists some definitions: "Place, in its literary sense, can be defined in several ways. For one thing, we may define place as the physical aspect of the environment at hand. In another sense, we may define place as the environment removed from the speaker or writer. In some instances, place is the term used to describe the setting in which issues of writing and other language-related skills are housed and discussed. In the literary world, place is usually combined with time and events to establish what is know [sic!] as the social setting or the social context of a literary work". Milford A. Jeremiah. "The Use of Place in Writing and Literature.", 23.

> place is commonly considered to be a smaller, more specific and local area that is characterized by its familiarity, the possibility of orientation and manageability.[34]

This observation reinforces that both terms are closely related and differ with respect to their size and knowability, which are two crucial aspects to distinguish between both terms. Given that such a general distinction will suffice for my analysis of Tolkien's *The Hobbit*, because the characteristics of 'place' will be more significant, I will adopt this differentiation. Throughout my book, I will thus use the term (narrative) place to refer to "an aspect of space, a smaller unit"[35] of space, which can be experienced by the characters of the story, whereas (narrative) space is seen as a much broader concept that "will be used in a more general sense as referring to an 'extended region'"[36]. This broad definition will enable me to draw upon ideas on place and/or space by scholars who do not differentiate between both terms at all.

In his article "Place", the social geographer T. Cresswell explores the notion and begins with the geographical sense of the word 'place': according to his definition, place "combines location, locale, and sense of place"[37]. While 'location' refers to a geographic position, the meaning of 'locale' is based on the tangible objects and features of the place, i.e. "the material setting"[38]. His last term, 'sense of place', describes "the feelings and emotions a place evokes"[39]. The connection with feelings and emotions emphasises that "[p]laces are not *per se* significant, they acquire meaning and value because we assign it to them"[40]. He furthermore argues that "[t]he sense of place evoked by fantasy novels, for instance, is usually based on a description of the material environs. Think of the hobbit holes of *The Lord of the Rings* or the magic staircases of *Hogwarts*"[41]. The importance of spatial relations in fantasy literature is indeed frequently linked with "a very strong sense of landscape"[42]. Nonetheless, the feelings and emotions associated with both natural and urban environments often depend on more than the description of the scenery.[43] They also result from the characters' point of view and their journeys: when reaching Weathertop, "Frodo for the first

---

34 Nicole Schröder. *Spaces and Places in Motion*, 45.

35 Ibid.

36 Ibid., 47.

37 T. Cresswell. "Place.", 169.

38 Ibid.

39 Ibid.

40 Nicole Schröder. *Spaces and Places in Motion*, 45, original emphasis.

41 T. Cresswell. "Place.", 169, original emphasis.

42 Colin Manlove, *The Fantasy Literature of England*, 1.

43 Zoran highlights this problem: "This set of concepts ['the classical dichotomy between *description* and *narration*, and its automatic parallelism with the pair *space* and *action*'] is to a great extent responsible for the false identification of space in the narrative with the descriptive sections, and for excluding *action* as well as most of the other components of the text from the phenomena relevant to space". Gabriel Zoran. "Towards a Theory of Space in Narrative.", 326, original emphasis.

time fully realized his homelessness and danger. He wished bitterly that his fortune had left him in the quiet and beloved Shire. He stared down at the hateful Road, leading back westward – to his home"[44]. It was only after Frodo had left his hobbit-hole and the Shire and was able to compare it to other places and spaces that he became aware of their importance and meaning for him.[45] Thus, Cresswell's 'sense of place' cannot only be used to describe the feelings evoked in the reader by means of description, but also, on a story-internal level, to elaborate on the character's attitudes towards certain places.

Given that "[t]he generation of space can also take place on a geographical scale, especially in stories structured as journeys or quests"[46], it is hardly surprising that the experience of places in literary texts is closely connected with the movements and perception of characters. This idea is also addressed in Wolfgang Hallet's and Birgit Neumann's introduction to *Raum und Bewegung in der Literatur*, in which they assume that spaces (in literary texts) are "humanly lived spaces"[47] ("menschlich erlebte Räume"[48]). Likewise, Sabine Buchholz and Manfred Jahn define narrative space in relation to movement and claim that "[a]t its most basic level, narrative space is the environment in which story-internal characters move about and live"[49]. In the context of the connections between place/space, movement and perspective, Anthony Pavlik claims that

> [t]he protagonists' [sic!] [or simply the character's] perceived spatial environment, the protagonist's self-location, depends upon the interrelations between perceptual experience of, and some form of purposeful interaction with, the perceived environment; that is, there is a context of basic spatial action and experience within the protagonist's perceived world.[50]

In his statement, he highlights the interdependence between the character's spatial actions, i.e., his or her movements and interactions within and between places, and the character's experiences, which influence his or her perception. Both aspects are essential constituents of the spatial construction and the (re-) negotiation of a character's identity. Therefore, it seems consequential that a space "is filled with memories and hopes"[51] when it is connected with experiences. On the one hand, characters shape their perception of a space when they interact with this space (e.g. by choosing to act in a particular way, or by placing objects). On the other hand, they can make individual connections that allow

44 J.R.R. Tolkien. *The Fellowship of the Ring*, 246.

45 This does not mean that Frodo did not assign feelings or emotions to the Shire before leaving it, but rather that the real importance of the Shire to him becomes apparent when he compares it to a different place.

46 H. Porter Abbott. *The Cambridge Introduction to Narrative*, 162.

47 My translation.

48 Wolfgang Hallet and Birgit Neumann. "Raum und Bewegung in der Literatur.", 11.

49 Sabine Buchholz and Manfred Jahn. "Space in Narrative", 552.

50 Anthony Pavlik. *A View from Elsewhere*, 7-8.

51 Ricardo Gullón. "On Space in the Novel.", 12.

them to recall particular events, i.e. their memories, which may evoke certain feelings and strengthen emotional ties that also change their perception of the space or place.

In children's literature, there is a long tradition of endowing place and space and specifically story-internal settings with significance:

> While settings from the oral tradition are usually generalized and vague, often no more than 'Once upon a time' followed by a scanty description of place (in a cottage or a palace, by the sea or in a forest), writers frequently use place and landscape as vital elements in their literature.[52]

A strong focus on place in literary texts for children can, for instance, be found in J.K. Rowling's description of Hogwarts in the *Harry Potter* series (1997-2007), C.S. Lewis' depictions of Charn and Narnia in *The Magician's Nephew* (1955) or with the Emerald City in L. Frank Baum's *The Wonderful Wizard of Oz* (1900). The significance of place and space is further enhanced by the fact that many stories written for children follow the "home/away/home pattern"[53], which allows the characters and the reader to consider 'home' (which is generally assumed to be safe but boring) and 'away' (which is held to be exciting but dangerous) as a binary opposition.[54] Although an opposition between places becomes most unambiguously apparent when they are binary oppositions, it is often already sufficient to show characters exploring a place that is different from the familiar ones to establish some form of distinction between them. This idea already implies that "[p]laces, too, are open and changing, related in permanent exchange to other places"[55].

The fact that places and spaces can change also suggests that they do not necessarily exist forever and can be transformed or even destroyed. As a result, characters often reproduce vanished or derelict places with the help of memories and material relics. It is important to note that this line of reasoning makes it a precondition that the characters had visited or inhabited this place prior to its destruction, which means that their points of view are highly subjective and that they associate certain feelings and emotions with its former state. If they reconstruct the place from memory, they are likely to even change certain aspects of

52 Marilyn Apseloff and Alethea Helbig. "Place in Children's Literature.", 9.

53 Perry Nodelman and Mavis Reimer. *The Pleasures of Children's Literature*, 197. The following examples use this pattern: the adventures of the Darling children in James M. Barrie's *Peter Pan* (1911), Lewis Carroll's *Alice's Adventures in Wonderland* (1865), the journeys of the Pevensie children from London to Narnia and back again in *The Lion, the Witch and the Wardrobe* by C.S. Lewis (1950), or Bilbo Baggins' journey from the Shire to Erebor and back to the Shire in J.R.R. Tolkien's *The Hobbit*.

54 Cf. Perry Nodelman and Mavis Reimer. *The Pleasures of Children's Literature*, 201. According to Ashcroft, Griffiths and Tiffin, "the binary opposition is the most extreme form of difference possible – sun/moon; man/woman; birth/death; black/white". "Binarism." in: Bill Ashcroft et al. *The Key Concepts*, 23.

55 Nicole Schröder. *Spaces and Places in Motion*, 46.

the original place. More dramatic changes will occur when their memories revolve around their home ("Heimat"[56]), which is frequently associated with nostalgic feelings[57] and which can be glorified or idealised to compensate for a feeling of loss.

The prevalence of the 'home/away/home pattern' also suggests that home as a place is especially common in children's literature.[58] Analysing 'home' in the context of the 'sanctuary topos', Jane Suzanne Carroll highlights the pivotal role of the home in relation to the individual:

> Providing a point at which the human body, the built environment and the natural landscape come together, the home is the site where the connection between human and landscape is at its most intense, where the boundaries between person and place, between the Self and the landscape, dissolve altogether.[59]

Home, thus, is an expression of the self, has been created by (human) beings or characters and is bound to a specific location. Her observation that "the connection between human and landscape is at its most intense" with respect to the home suggests that this place is typically connected with very strong emotions.[60] The prevalence of 'home' in children's stories led Lucy Waddey to identify three patterns that have emerged: "Although so deep and subtle a subject as home eludes any final categories, the artistic use of home as both a setting and theme in children's fiction falls into three basic patterns: home as a frame, home as a focus, and home as an evolving reflection of the protagonist"[61]. These three patterns, which she names the 'Odyssean pattern', the 'Oedipal pattern' and the 'Promethean pattern',[62] illustrate how differently home can be negotiated in stories for children and which functions and uses can be assigned to it. With focus on the stories by Beatrix Potter, Waddey explains that in stories following the 'Odyssean pattern' (which essentially adheres to the "home/away/home pattern"[63]) "home is also usually an important theme. The characters in such books romanticize their homes; their memories invest the simplest hut with rich

---

56 Friederike Eigler. *Heimat, Space, Narrative*, 22.

57 Cf. ibid.

58 Cf. Perry Nodelman and Mavis Reimer. *The Pleasures of Children's Literature*, 197-98.

59 Jane Suzanne Carroll. *Landscape in Children's Literature*, 20.

60 In their article "Goodbye Yellow Brick Road: Challenging the Mythology of Home in Children's Literature", Melissa B. Wilson and Kathy G. Short draw attention to the fact that home does not necessarily have to evoke pleasant memories or positive feelings: "Home has traditionally been a place where the child protagonist is cared for, loved, and disciplined while waiting to become an adult. Generally, it is the beginning and end of a children's story. This is not to say that home is not problematic – it often is". Melissa B. Wilson and Kathy G. Short. "Goodbye Yellow Brick Road: Challenging the Mythology of Home in Children's Literature.", 130.

61 Lucy Waddey. "Home in Children's Fiction.", 13.

62 Cf. ibid., 13-15.

63 Perry Nodelman and Mavis Reimer. *The Pleasures of Children's Literature*, 197.

beauty, because there they are safe and there they truly belong"[64]. Stories in which "home is the beginning, middle, and end, an objective reality, a place where important things happen, unromanticized by distance"[65], follow the 'Oedipal pattern'. Finally, stories that "begin with no representation of home at all, but with the protagonist as a kind of exile"[66] and where "the characters have left one home and, usually through a good deal of work, create another"[67] follow the 'Promethean pattern'.[68] In J.R.R. Tolkien's *The Hobbit*, the notion of home does not only serve as a framing device of the adventure but is also one of the story's main themes. Given that the hobbit's experience of home differs from that of the homeless dwarves, the subsequent subchapter will further elaborate on the notion of home and focus on 'home' and 'belonging' in the context of diaspora.

1.2 Diasporic Space

Nostalgic feelings, a lost home and a sense of belonging are key aspects of the term 'diaspora', which is to be found in the field of postcolonial studies. Although the term was "[f]irst used to describe the Jewish dispersion in Babylonian times"[69], it has been picked up by scholars in postcolonial studies to refer to similar dispersions. Avtar Brah claims that "[a]t the heart of the notion of diaspora is the image of a journey"[70]. While this statement does not provide a clear definition of the term, it contains an important idea: a (large) group of people move from one place to another.

A more precise definition of the term 'diaspora' is provided by Justin D. Edwards, who uses the biblical term[71] in the context of postcolonialism and claims: "Diaspora, then, is a word used in postcolonial studies to describe groups of people who have been removed or displaced due to territorial disputes, war,

---

64 Lucy Waddey. "Home in Children's Fiction.", 13.

65 Ibid.

66 Ibid., 14.

67 Ibid.

68 It should be noted that Lucy Waddey does not see these patterns as mutually exclusive; instead, they can all "be present in some degree, enriching and expanding the reader's perceptions of himself and his own attitudes toward home". Ibid., 15.

69 Bill Ashcroft et al. "Diaspora.", 425.

70 Avtar Brah. "Thinking through the Concept of Diaspora.", 443.

71 Tobias Döring explains its origin as follows: the term "is traditionally used with reference to Jewish history where it describes the experience [...] of living outside the Holy Land: in foreign countries, with sometimes hostile host societies and often under acute forms of oppression". Tobias Döring. *Postcolonial Literatures in English*, 30. Ashcroft, Griffiths and Tiffin also say that "the term has its origins in the Jewish diaspora", but they add that the modern meaning of the term was influenced by imperialism. Bill Ashcroft et al. "Diaspora.", 426.

forced migration or immigration"[72]. In this definition, the 'journey' is replaced by a political, military or social confrontation. He describes the forced movement of groups and enumerates four reasons. Conflicts, such as "territorial disputes" and "war", can arise between peoples or, since colonial times, between coloniser and colonised. The third term, "forced migration", contains a political undertone and can refer to people fleeing to escape persecution. The fourth term, "immigration", seems to be more neutral because the immigration of a group can have various causes, such as political, social or economic problems.

Bill Ashcroft, Gareth Griffiths and Helen Tiffin go one step further and state that 'immigration' is connected with journeys from one country to another, whereas the term 'diaspora' (from Greek διασπορά, "*a scattering, dispersion*"[73]) describes "the scattering throughout the world from one geographic location"[74], i.e. from a homeland. This indicates that each immigrant usually arrives at a clearly defined destination after his or her journey, whereas the word 'diaspora' expresses the dispersion of a people – their destinations are secondary. They even claim that 'diaspora' means 'exile', which is (in the Bible) often a punishment.[75] According to Ashcroft, Griffiths and Tiffin, this dispersion "leads to a splitting in the sense of home"[76]: "the society of relocation"[77] versus "a homeland that is connected to language, religion and a sense of cultural belonging"[78]. In other words, the term 'diaspora' is connected with the scattering of a people and, consequently, their handling of their new situation in a different country.

The spatial distance leads James Clifford to contend that "[d]iaspora cultures thus mediate, in a lived tension, the experiences of separation and entanglement, of living here and remembering/desiring another place"[79]. Interestingly, he uses the term 'desiring' and hints at a yearning or longing for a place which exists in reality but that is distant; it "is the sense of living in one country but looking across time and space to another"[80]. This makes the distant homeland a construct because "[i]t [home] exists primarily in the mind"[81]. The reconstruction of his or her home is dependent on the individual's experiences and memories. It is thus important to become aware of how they remember their original home and how the mental picture survives in their collective memory because their home has vital functions:

72 Justin D. Edwards. *Postcolonial Literature*, 150.

73 "Diaspora" in: Henry G. Liddell et al. *A Greek-English Lexicon*, 359, original emphasis.

74 Bill Ashcroft et al. "Diaspora.", 425.

75 Cf. ibid.

76 Ibid.

77 Ibid.

78 Justin D. Edwards. *Postcolonial Literature*, 150.

79 James Clifford. "Diasporas.", 453.

80 John McLeod. *Beginning Postcolonialism*, 237.

81 Ibid., 241.

It can act as a valuable means of orientation by giving us a fixed, reliable sense of our place in the world. It is meant to tell us where we originated from and apparently where we legitimately belong. As an *idea* it stands for shelter, stability, security and comfort (although actual experiences of home may well fail to deliver these promises).[82]

These functions and meanings of the term 'home' already indicate why individuals typically feel a stronger emotional connection with their home than with any other place they temporarily inhabit or experience. A good example to illustrate this strong and special bond between the individual and his or her home can be found in Salman Rushdie's essay "Imaginary Homelands", in which he describes his own diasporic experiences.

Born in India, Rushdie moved to England as a young man, where he wrote his novel *Midnight's Children* (1981) and reflected on his childhood home, which he pictured in his mind with the help of a black-and-white photograph on a wall of the room where he worked.[83] After he had visited the actual house in the photograph, Rushdie became aware that he tended to see his own past, his childhood, as a monochromatic world, and he realised "how much [...] [he] wanted to restore the past to [...] [himself], not in the faded greys of old family-album snapshots, but whole, in CinemaScope and glorious Technicolor"[84]. Rushdie recognised the importance of his home, even though it was "a lost home in a lost city in the mists of lost time"[85], and he noticed that he "had a city and a history to reclaim"[86]. Despite being able to visit his home city Mumbai, he still cannot travel back into the past: instead of focusing on the present, however, he has a great interest in his past, or, more precisely, the memory of his former home, which he wants to revive. Yet, the mental image of his home is "built from the incomplete odds and ends of memory that [...] [have] survive[d] from the past"[87]. His memory is a collection of fragments, which are highly subjective and linked with his experiences and the (reconstructed) perspective of the young Salman Rushdie. Rushdie believes:

It may be that writers in my position, exiles or emigrants or expatriates, are haunted by some sense of loss, some urge to reclaim, to look back, even at the risk of being mutated into pillars of salt. But if we do look back, we must also do so in the knowledge – which gives rise to profound uncertainties – that our physical alienation from India almost inevitably means that we will not be capable of reclaiming precisely the thing that was lost; that we will, in short, create fictions, not actual cities or villages, but invisible ones, imaginary homelands, Indias of the mind.[88]

---

82 John McLeod. *Beginning Postcolonialism*, 242, original emphasis.

83 Cf. Salman Rushdie. "Imaginary Homelands.", 9.

84 Ibid., 9-10.

85 Ibid., 9.

86 Ibid., 10.

87 John McLeod. *Beginning Postcolonialism*, 243.

88 Salman Rushdie. "Imaginary Homelands.", 10. This view is shared by Avtar Brah, who states that "'home' is a mythic place of desire in the diasporic imagination. In this sense

These "fictions", as he calls them, produce their own "version"[89] of his home by evoking specific and vivid memories, while other vital aspects connected with a physical space are lacking altogether because they have simply been forgotten. Rushdie highlights the above-mentioned fragmentation and says: "fragmentation made trivial things seem like symbols, and the mundane acquired numinous qualities"[90]. That is, misperceptions and glorifications play a significant role in rebuilding the imaginary, lost home.

The connections between memories, fictions and nostalgia in a postcolonial context were also analysed by Dennis Walder, who highlights the relationship between "[m]emory and fictional creation"[91] and states that a feeling of nostalgia lies somewhere in between.[92] In spite of the many different definitions of 'nostalgia', "the yearning for a different and previous time/place/experience remains fundamental"[93]. Svetlana Boym states that the term "[n]ostalgia (from *nostos* – return home, and *algia* – longing) is a longing for a home that no longer exists or has never existed. Nostalgia is a sentiment of loss and displacement, but it is also a romance with one's own fantasy"[94]. Her comment suggests that nostalgia is often linked with past and present situations that are vital in evoking nostalgic feelings. Fred Davis argues along similar lines and emphasises that "more than 'mere past' is involved [in evoking nostalgic feelings]. It is a past imbued with special qualities which acquires its significance from the particular way we juxtapose it to certain features of our present lives"[95]. He further elaborates on the nostalgic experience and claims that "the nostalgic feeling is infused with sentiments of past beauty, pleasure, joy, satisfaction, goodness, happiness, love, etc.; in sum, any or several of the *positive* affects of being"[96] and foregrounds the emotional basis. In this context, it is crucial to acknowledge that "[t]he logic of nostalgia dictates that nothing can really be recovered, only re-collected, re-imagined"[97], which reinforces that the gap between past and pre-

---

it is a place of no-return, even if it is possible to visit the geographical territory that is seen as the place of 'origin'". Qtd. in: John McLeod. *Beginning Postcolonialism*, 241.

89 Salman Rushdie. "Imaginary Homelands.", 10.

90 Ibid., 12. Rushdie acknowledges his highly subjective view on India when he states: "'[M]y' India, a version and no more than one version of all the hundreds of millions of possible versions". Ibid., 10.

91 Dennis Walder. *Postcolonial Nostalgias*, 7.

92 Cf. ibid.

93 Ibid., 9.

94 Svetlana Boym. *The Future of Nostalgia*, xiii, original emphasis. By contrast, Fred Davis traces the origin of the term back to "the Greek *nostos*, to return home, and *algai*, a painful condition", which makes it "a painful yearning to return home". Fred Davis. "Nostalgia, Identity and the Current Nostalgia Wave.", 414, original emphasis.

95 Fred Davis. "Nostalgia, Identity and the Current Nostalgia Wave.", 418.

96 Ibid., original emphasis.

97 S.D. Chrostowska "Consumed by Nostalgia?", 54.

sent is irreconcilable and that nostalgia is directed to a past state that can never be reached (again).

Walder states that the "use of remembering"[98] can be found in diverse "literary or quasi-literary forms, in poetry and song, drama and story-telling – not to mention photography and film, where the role of nostalgia has been immense"[99]. Although Walder focuses on writers and their narrative texts, his statements are also true in the narrated world, in which characters can act as writers or storytellers, or can sing songs. When certain topics are evoked in these stories or songs – such as melancholy, a yearning or a longing for a homeland, to name but a few – nostalgia is expressed through them.[100] By contrast, the way that diasporic characters imagine their own home shapes their identity, and their identity determines how they act in and react to specific situations. Moreover, because the diasporic movements always imply the movement of a large group of people, "[n]ostalgia and national identity are inextricably entwined"[101]. That is, a song full of nostalgia, which is sung in the diegetic reality, can be a source of personal and/or collective identity (for the characters). In other words, the term 'nostalgia' also describes the feeling of missing a home, and this feeling can affect an individual or an entire community – even though the home might only be a memory.[102]

In my analysis, I will consider 'diaspora' as a situation in which individuals or groups have to leave their home country for one of several reasons and live in a country that they do not consider their home. In this context, it is crucial to take into consideration that "[m]igrants tend to arrive in new places with baggage; both in the physical sense of possessions or belongings, but also the less tangible matter of beliefs, traditions, customs, behaviours and values"[103]. These beliefs, traditions and values become a vital part of their definition of 'home' and consequently have an impact on identity and identity construction. John McLeod observes that the "disjunction between past and present, between here and there, makes 'home' seem far-removed in time and space, available for return only through an act of the imagination"[104]. While they are forced to live in a foreign country, they are also alienated from their homeland, which, being a special place, is connected with the words 'origin' and 'belonging'.

Robin Cohen says that "'the old country' – a notion often buried deep in language, religion, custom or folklore – always has some claim on their [diasporic

98 Dennis Walder. *Postcolonial Nostalgias*, 6.

99 Ibid.

100 Cf. ibid., 4-6.

101 Ibid., 5. In this respect, Boym goes a step further and maintains that "[u]nlike melancholia, which confines itself to the planes of individual consciousness, nostalgia is about the relationship between individual biography and the biography of groups or nations, between personal and collective memory". Svetlana Boym. *The Future of Nostalgia*, xvi.

102 Cf. Dennis Walder. *Postcolonial Nostalgias*, 4-5.

103 John McLeod. *Beginning Postcolonialism*, 244.

104 Ibid., 243.

individuals'] loyalty and emotions"[105]. For example, as explained above, migrants create and depend on imaginary homelands, which are based on past experiences in their real homeland, and which evoke strong feelings and emotions. These imaginary homelands are created from all their memories, which can be traumatic, such as times of suffering, as well as pleasant and mere fragments. Their perceptions of their homes and their homeland can vary and change drastically, though they often tend to idealise these homes. Ultimately, the diasporic individuals "[live] loss and hope as a defining tension"[106]. On the one hand, the loss of their home has left deep scars, and this lost home still exists in their imagination. On the other hand, they live in the hope of returning to their lost home and of restoring it to its former state.

105 Qtd. in: John McLeod. *Beginning Postcolonialism*, 237.
106 James Clifford. "Diasporas.", 454.

PART II: THE DWARF KINGDOM

2.1 A Brief Introduction to the Depiction of Dwarves in Tolkien's Writings

> 'Long ago in my grandfather Thror's time our family was driven out of the far North, and came back with all their wealth and their tools to this Mountain on the map [Erebor]. It had been discovered by my far ancestor, Thrain the Old, but now they mined and they tunnelled and they made huger halls and greater workshops – and in addition I believe they found a good deal of gold and a great many jewels too.'[107]

From Thorin's retrospective account of the former dwarf kingdom and its expansion, the reader can draw many conclusions about the nature of Tolkien's dwarves. They are not only wealthy and associated with riches in the form of gold and jewels, but they are also connected with craftsmanship and skill as well as with subterranean abodes. Precisely because these issues are also connected with dwarves more generally, scholars claim that Tolkien's fiction tends to "[combine] ancient source material with idiosyncratic preference"[108]. Tolkien himself stated that the depiction of his dwarves is based on folklore and Germanic legends but is "still in many ways very different from them"[109], which makes the analysis of Tolkien's dwarves within his Middle-earth universe particularly promising.

In this context, it is crucial to acknowledge that Tolkien creates the dwarves in Middle-earth and in his other stories rather inconsistently. With focus on Tolkien's early stories ('The Nauglafring', 'Beren and Lúthien', 'Túrin' and 'The Coming of Men'), John D. Rateliff explains that "[t]hroughout these early stories they [the dwarves] are viewed exclusively from an (unflattering) elvish perspective"[110] and that *The Hobbit* presents a more positive image of this people. This change in representation already implies the dwarves' growing significance in both *The Hobbit* and *The Lord of the Rings* (1954-55).[111] By endowing them with more positive characteristics and by depicting them as a people that is fond of music and food, Tolkien paved the way for the alliance between dwarves and the other free peoples of Middle-earth, whose representa-

---

107 J.R.R. Tolkien. *The Hobbit*, 27-28.

108 Paul Acker, Matthew Bardowell and Jeffrey A. Weinstock. "Dwarf.", 199. They further note that this can be seen in Tolkien's plural of the word 'dwarf'. Cf. ibid.

109 Humphrey Carpenter. *Letters of J.R.R. Tolkien*, 383 [Letter 297: Drafts for a Letter to 'Mr Rang', August 1967].

110 John D. Rateliff. *The History of The Hobbit*, 76. Referring to Rateliff's "Anchoring the Myth – The Impact of *The Hobbit* on Tolkien's Legendarium", Bradford Lee Eden points out that "[i]n the previous 'Silmarillion' material, dwarves are presented as prone to evil if not outright evil, treacherous, and avaricious", which reinforces their negative portrayal. Bradford Lee Eden. "Introduction.", 1.

111 Renée Vink also sees the more positive depiction of Gimli as a marker for change: "However, Tolkien's image of Dwarves improved markedly in *The Lord of the Rings* because of the picture he paints of their chief representative in the epic, Gimli son of Glóin". Renée Vink. "'Jewish' Dwarves: Tolkien and Anti-Semitic Stereotyping.", 128.

tives eventually form the Fellowship of the Ring.[112] Gerard Hynes elaborates on the different versions of Tolkien's dwarves and claims that "[t]heir depiction in *The Hobbit* as proud, honorable, and ultimately dependable is a remarkable development"[113], which highlights that the children's story "may mark a point where Tolkien began to engage more critically with his sources, presenting dwarves as honorable rather than merely mercenary"[114].

In appendix F to *The Lord of the Rings*, Tolkien states that his "small, stout and bearded"[115] people are "lovers of stone, of gems, of things that take shape under the hands of the craftsman rather than things that live by their own life"[116]. This strong focus on craftsmanship, which is also partially addressed in Thorin's retrospective account, can be traced back to *The Silmarillion* (1977), in which the origins, or to be more precise, the creation of the dwarves is addressed. Renée Vink even argues that "[t]he Dwarves are also given a creation story of their own"[117]. They were created by the Vala[118] Aulë, who "is a smith and a master of all crafts, and he delights in works of skill, however small"[119]. Apparently, he served as the role model for his own creation, which is the reason why the dwarves share his 'profession'; with focus on the depiction of Gimli in *The Lord of the Rings*, Michael N. Stanton notes that "[w]e may suppose that like all Dwarves, Gimli is a craftsman, or metal-smith, or perhaps a stoneworker of great skill"[120], thus enumerating some of the 'professions' of the dwarves. But the dwarves also retained other features that are associated with their creator, such as their love of gold and gems. It is said that "[h]is [Aulë's] are the gems that lie deep in the Earth and the gold that is fair in the hand, no less than the walls of the mountains and the basins of the sea"[121]. Thus, from the beginning of their creation, the dwarves have been closely connected with crafts and skills as well as a desire for gems and gold. Eventually, this combination arguably con-

---

112 Michael N. Stanton remarks that "Dwarves mark one of the strongest elements of continuity between *The Hobbit* and *The Lord of the Rings*". Michael N. Stanton. *Hobbits, Elves, and Wizards*, 108. For a more detailed account on the changing perception of dwarves see John D. Rateliff. "Anchoring the Myth – The Impact of *The Hobbit* on Tolkien's Legendarium." 6-19; and Gerard Hynes. "From Nauglath to Durin's Folk – *The Hobbit* and Tolkien's Dwarves.", 20-37.

113 Gerard Hynes. "From Nauglath to Durin's Folk.", 20.

114 Ibid.

115 "Dwarves." in: J.E.A. Tyler. *The Tolkien Companion*, 121.

116 J.R.R. Tolkien. *The Return of the King*, 1488.

117 Renée Vink. "'Jewish' Dwarves: Tolkien an Anti-Semitic Stereotyping.",125.

118 According to Tyler, the 'Valar' (sg. Vala) are "[t]he Guardians of the World", who participated in the creation of Middle-earth. "Valar." in: J.E.A. Tyler. *The Tolkien Companion*, 502.

119 J.R.R. Tolkien. *The Silmarillion*, 17-18.

120 Michael N. Stanton. *Hobbits, Elves, and Wizards*, 108. In his song about Moria, Gimli also refers to the dwarves as masons and miners and more indirectly as goldsmiths. Cf. J.R.R. Tolkien. *The Fellowship of the Ring*, 412.

121 J.R.R. Tolkien. *The Silmarillion*, 18.

tributed to the dwarves' creation of precious and famous objects, which are mentioned repeatedly in *The Hobbit.*

According to Thorin's statement (quoted at the beginning of this chapter), the dwarves live within the mountain itself.[122] After Ilúvatar found out what Aulë created without his permission, he concludes that the dwarves "shall sleep now in the darkness under stone"[123] until it is their time to come into being, which explains the dwarves' preference for dark places.[124] With the foundation of the dwarf kingdom by Thorin's ancestor Thrain the Old, the dwarves transformed the mountain in their own fashion, yet still live "under stone"[125]. This transformation includes the reshaping of the mountain's interior: "'they mined and they tunnelled and they made huger halls and greater workshops'"[126]. Thus they created their own social and cultural space within the protective walls of the mountain. This location in the mountain is strategically well chosen, because it is "easily defended (except against Dragons)", as Tyler remarks, "but – more important to the Dwarves – it [...] [is] also exceedingly rich in minerals and precious metals"[127]. These minerals and metals are both the cause for the prosperity of the dwarf kingdom and the reason for the dragon attack. More than once in Tolkien's Middle-earth dwarf kingdoms have been attacked by dragons and their inhabitants have been forced to seek another homeland.[128]

2.2 Collective Memory and the Reconstruction of Erebor

In the first part of Peter Jackson's adaptation *An Unexpected Journey*, the frame narrative of Bilbo Baggins refers to the dispersal of the dwarves, which resembles a diasporic movement. After Smaug conquered the dwarf kingdom, the dwarves meander through a barren land, disperse in the world and are, as Bilbo's voice-over puts it, "'[r]obbed of their homeland'"[129]. The harsh contrast between the mighty and glorious dwarf kingdom and the withered land emphasises the dwarves' loss of home even more strongly.[130] However, it is not only

---

122 Paul Acker, Matthew Bardowell and Jeffrey A. Weinstock acknowledge that even in folklore dwarfs dwell in hollow mountains, as in the Brothers Grimm's fairy tale "Snow White and the Seven Dwarfs". Cf. Paul Acker, Matthew Bardowell and Jeffrey A. Weinstock. "Dwarf.", 199.

123 J.R.R. Tolkien. *The Silmarillion*, 38.

124 In *The Hobbit*, Thorin and his companions also express their preference for darkness, even if with a slightly different focus: "'We like the dark, [...] [d]ark for dark business!'". J.R.R. Tolkien. *The Hobbit*, 20.

125 J.R.R. Tolkien. *The Silmarillion*, 38.

126 J.R.R. Tolkien. *The Hobbit*, 27.

127 "Erebor." in: J.E.A. Tyler. *The Tolkien Companion*, 158.

128 Cf. J.R.R. Tolkien. *The Return of the King*, 1407.

129 Peter Jackson. *An Unexpected Journey*, 00:07:38-00:07:40.

130 Peter Jackson's adaptation shows an almost flat plain that is encircled by mountains. It features lakes of varying sizes, which contrast the withering brown surrounding. In be-

Jackson's adaptation which conveys the idea of diaspora, but also Tolkien's history of the dwarves more generally.[131] In his appendices to *The Lord of the Rings*, Tolkien describes, among other things, also the history of the dwarves and reinforces their diasporic situation.

From a 'historical' point of view, the dwarves have been subject to many involuntary movements in Middle-earth. In the First Age, there were three great dwarf cities: Nogrod and Belegost in the Blue Mountains and Moria, or Khazad-dûm as the dwarves call it in their own language, in the Misty Mountains.[132] They were considered to be three of the great dwellings of the dwarves, of which Moria is best known, as its founder Durin was the "eldest and most royal of all the Seven Fathers of the Dwarves"[133]. Nogrod and Belegost, however, were destroyed at the end of the First Age already. The subsequent movement of the dwarves forms the basis on which Tyler argues that "many dispossessed Dwarves of those cities flocked to Khazâd-dûm"[134], which is a statement that hints at two vital ideas connected with diaspora. On the one hand, the dwarves are dispossessed of their homeland due to "the breaking of Thangorodrim"[135] in "the Great Battle"[136], in which Belegost and Nogrod have been ruined.[137] On the other hand, the kingdoms' former inhabitants "flocked" to Moria. Hence, it was a movement of people who were expelled from their original homeland and were forced to take refuge with their relatives. This kind of movement, however, is rather unusual in the context of diaspora, because they move as a group to another dwelling instead of splitting into smaller groups and being scattered across the world. Although this movement led to an increase of Moria's inhabi-

---

tween the lakes, the former inhabitants of Erebor make their way through the plain by walking around the lakes with their belongings and animals. When the camera zooms out, the size of the plain can be seen and the substantial number of dwarves that survived the dragon's attack and lost their home is emphasised. Cf. Peter Jackson. *An Unexpected Journey*, 00:07:38.

131 Cf. Humphrey Carpenter. *Letters of J.R.R. Tolkien*, 229 [Letter 176: From a letter to Naomi Mitchison, 8 December 1955]. John Rateliff also elaborates on the comparison between Jews and the dwarves and uses Tolkien's 1965 BBC interview with Denys Gueroult as a basis for his argumentation, which suggests even more strongly that Tolkien was aware of these parallels. Cf. John D. Rateliff. *The History of The Hobbit*, 79-80.

132 Cf. J.R.R. Tolkien. *The Return of the King*, 1406.; cf. "Moria." in: J.E.A. Tyler. *The Tolkien Companion*, 313-14.

133 "Dwarves." in: J.E.A. Tyler. *The Tolkien Companion*, 117.

134 Ibid. In "The Quest of Erebor" (1980), in which Tolkien elaborates on the further movements of the dwarves, he states that some of them returned to Moria after they had been driven out of Erebor, whereas Thráin set out from the Ered Luin (the Blue Mountains) to reclaim Erebor. Cf. J.R.R. Tolkien. "The Quest of Erebor.", 415.

135 J.R.R. Tolkien. *The Return of the King*, 1406.

136 "War of the Great Jewels." in: J.E.A. Tyler. *The Tolkien Companion*, 513.

137 Cf. "Belegost." in: J.E.A. Tyler. *The Tolkien Companion*, 56. Edwards, for instance, highlights that war is among the reasons for diasporic movements. Cf. Justin D. Edwards. *Postcolonial Literature*, 150.

tants, crafts and wealth, the great kingdom of the dwarves was destroyed by a Balrog in the Third Age, which establishes a link with two other aspects of diaspora that are emphasised by Ashcroft, Griffiths and Tiffin, namely punishment and exile.[138] When the dwarves of Moria further expanded their kingdom, they found the most precious metal mithril, on which they based their wealth.[139] However, the dwarves "'delved too greedily and too deep'", as Gandalf explains, "'and disturbed that from which they fled, Durin's Bane [the Balrog of Morgoth]'"[140]. Thus, the Balrog can be seen as an immediate punishment for the dwarves' greed. This destruction finally led to the first actual scattering through the world, since some of the dwarves made their way to Erebor, while others went to the Grey Mountains.[141]

Similar to the explanation given for the Balrog, Peter Jackson's movie adaptation puts the attack on Erebor, contrary to its description in the novel, down to the dwarves. *The Hobbit* and appendix A of *The Lord of the Rings* indicate that Smaug the Golden ransacked the mountain because "the rumour of the wealth of Erebor spread abroad"[142], whereas the movie version suggests that the dragon was the immediate punishment for finding and taking the Arkenstone, the Heart of the Mountain.[143] This idea is affirmed on the temporal level: although more than 700 years passed between the finding of the Arkenstone and the coming of the dragon, the movie indicates that it was only a matter of time before the dragon attacked the mountain, which supports the assumption that his coming was a punishment. While Tolkien focused primarily on the dragon's greedy nature as the reason for Smaug's attack on Erebor, the adaptation provides a slightly different emphasis by making the dwarves' desire for gold and gemstones (and to some extent also the dragon's greed) the reason of the attack.

Notwithstanding this shift in interpretation, the dwarves are presented as a 'wandering folk' in both the novel and the adaptation. In his prose account of the destruction of the dwarf kingdom in Erebor, Thorin concludes: "'we went away, and we have had to earn our livings as best we could up and down the lands, often enough sinking as low as blacksmith-work or even coalmining. But

138 Cf. Bill Ashcroft et al. "Diaspora.", 425.

139 Cf. J.R.R. Tolkien. *The Fellowship of the Ring*, 413.

140 Ibid. In appendix A to *The Lord of the Rings*, Tolkien also hints at the possibility that the Balrog had already been "released from prison", as "it may well be that it had already been awakened by the malice of Sauron". J.R.R. Tolkien. *The Return of the King*, 1407, n.2.

141 Cf. J.R.R. Tolkien. *The Return of the King*, 1407. After the Grey Mountains had been attacked by a cold-drake, its inhabitants went back to Erebor or to the Iron Hills, which highlights the idea of the wandering folk. Cf. ibid.

142 Ibid., 1408.

143 In Jackson's adaptation, Bilbo's voice-over emphasises this idea by saying: "'But the years of peace and plenty were not to last. Slowly the days turned sour and the watchful nights closed in'", which suggests that the attack of the dragon was only a matter of days or years. Peter Jackson. *An Unexpected Journey*, 00:03:44-00:03:54.

we have never forgotten our stolen treasure'"[144]. His statement highlights that the dwarves were unable to find a new permanent settlement and that they remained in motion "'up and down the lands'". Thorin's use of the first person plural, 'we', emphasises that this statement is meant to refer to the entire group of dwarves. In addition, the dwarves have never forgotten their treasure, which can be seen allegorically for their homeland, and which is the reason why they reunite and attempt to reclaim Erebor.[145]

As indicated at the beginning of the chapter, the idea of the diaspora can also be traced in the choice of words with which the attack on Erebor is described in Tolkien's works, especially in the appendices to *The Lord of the Rings*. A first example, in which the choice of words is striking, is the description of the events following the dragon's attack when Thror and Thrain came through the secret door and went with their family and some of their kinsmen south "into long and homeless wandering"[146]. The choice of words already indicates that Erebor became their home and that every other dwelling is nothing but "just a stage in transit, a provisional abode before returning to the true homeland"[147]. This aspect is enhanced by the term "wandering", which suggests neither a clear destination, nor a permanent settlement somewhere else. This idea is also addressed in Tyler's *The Tolkien Companion*, in which he uses the terms "scattered", "dispossessed" and "dispersed" to describe the dwarves' situation.[148] A second instance in which the choice of words plays a significant role is when the narrator points out that "Thráin and Thorin with what remained of their following [...] returned to Dunland, and soon afterwards they removed and wandered in Eriador, until at last they *made a home in exile* in the east of the Ered Luin beyond the Lune"[149]. As Justin D. Edwards remarks with focus on postcolonial

144 J.R.R. Tolkien. *The Hobbit*, 30.

145 Moreover, in Peter Jackson's *An Unexpected Journey*, Bilbo (in form of a voice-over) stresses that Thorin also did not forget the attack on the mountain: "'But always he remembered the mountain smoke beneath the moon, the trees like torches blazing bright. For he had seen dragon fire in the sky and a city turned to ash. And he never forgave and he never forgot'". Peter Jackson. *An Unexpected Journey*, 00:07:56-00:08:15.

146 J.R.R. Tolkien. *The Return of the King*, 1408.

147 Tobias Döring. *Postcolonial Literatures in English*, 31. Döring makes this remark in the context of Jewish history; he claims that retaining certain elements connected with Jewish life is only possible when viewing the diaspora as a journey that ends in the return to the homeland.

148 Cf. "Dwarves." in: J.E.A. Tyler. *The Tolkien Companion*, 118. William Kircher, the actor who played Bifur, uses these or similar terms to describe the dwarves' situation: "About two hundred years ago, Smaug killed thousands of our ancestors and took our kingdom. As a result, we were dispossessed and went off in different directions into exile, since then we have been trying to survive, eking out a living as best we can. Now, the Dwarvish race is gradually diminishing so our desire to take back Erebor is about reclaiming our racial identity and what we feel is spiritually ours by right. That's why we're up for the fight". Qtd. in: Brian Sibley. *The Desolation of Smaug – Official Movie Guide*, 38.

149 J.R.R. Tolkien. *The Return of the King*, 1413, my emphasis.

literature, the "homeland [...] is connected to language, religion and a sense of cultural belonging"[150]. In a similar vein, the dwarf language Khuzdul remained a secret language of the dwarves. Although they usually spoke the languages of those among whom they dwelt or with whom they traded, their own language was considered a language of lore and was guarded "as a treasure of the past"[151]. Finally, the choice of words is relevant when Tolkien states that "in their songs they [the dwarves] spoke ever of the Lonely Mountain far away"[152]. On the one hand, it confirms John McLeod's statement that people in diaspora are "living in one country but [...] [look] across time and space to another"[153], namely to the place they desire most: their home. For the dwarves, the Lonely Mountain is at first predominantly geographically distant, while over the years and decades it becomes also temporally distant, so that it only exists in their memories. On the other hand, the song shapes their (collective) identity, because songs are not only a means of expressing community; they are often performed by a group of people and are partly the reason for and expression of the dwarves' communal spirit on their quest to reclaim Erebor.

Thus, the history of the dwarves shows that they have been exposed to involuntary movements and expulsion several times and for several reasons.[154] Michael N. Stanton observes that "[i]n the summer before Frodo's fiftieth birthday, strange events included the news that a large number of Dwarves were moving along the old East-West Road that crossed the Shire"[155], which points to the fact that the dwarves' movements have not ceased after the dwarves of Erebor reclaimed their homeland. This idea is further consolidated by the description in *The Lord of the Rings* in which the narrator points out that "Frodo often met strange dwarves of far countries, *seeking refuge* in the West. They were troubled, and some spoke in whispers of the Enemy and of the Land of Mordor"[156].

The diasporic situation of the dwarves in Tolkien's children's novel allows arguing that they (at the beginning of *The Hobbit*) are situated "in a lived tension, the experiences of separation and entanglement, of living here and remembering/desiring another place"[157]. This desire is articulated in the 'Song of the Lonely Mountain', which they sing in Bilbo's hobbit-hole and which explains the dwarves' quest and their motivation to embark on the journey. This song,

---

150 Justin D. Edwards. *Postcolonial Literature*, 150.

151 J.R.R. Tolkien. *The Return of the King*, 1488.

152 Ibid., 1415.

153 John McLeod. *Beginning Postcolonialism*, 243.

154 In the records of "The Quest of Erebor", Thorin informs Gandalf that "'Dwarves have had more dealings with Dragons than most, and you are not instructing the ignorant'". J.R.R. Tolkien. "The Quest of Erebor.", 430. This utterance hints at the fact that Smaug was not the first dragon the dwarves encountered and that they probably had to defend their homelands more than once against a dragon.

155 Michael N. Stanton. *Hobbits, Elves, and Wizards*, 107.

156 J.R.R. Tolkien. *The Fellowship of the Ring*, 57, my emphasis.

157 James Clifford. "Diasporas.", 453.

which has been deemed to give the best introduction to the dwarves,[158] refers to their present situation and their former lives as smiths and craftsmen under the mountain.

In her analysis of songs in Tolkien's *The Lord of the Rings*, Amy M. Amendt-Raduege claims that "[t]he songs and stories of Middle-earth [...] promote immortality in a different form: they serve as foci for communal commemoration, and thus locate immortality within culture itself"[159]. The 'Song of the Lonely Mountain' is used with a similar purpose, as it commemorates the former dwarf kingdom and the dragon's attack. When Bilbo Baggins hears this song for the first time, he is still in his comfortable hobbit-hole. Deeply touched by the song, he is "swept away into dark lands under strange moons, far over The Water and very far from his hobbit-hole under The Hill"[160]. This may be one of the reasons why Mark Atherton claims that the song reveals even more information than Thorin's subsequent prose explanation.[161] Since the song is a medium that is associated with remembering,[162] it is no coincidence that the overall topic of the song is the yearning for a lost kingdom. It highlights that "[t]he songs and stories of Middle-earth [...] tell us something significant about its themes, both about what is remembered and what is worth remembering. Each of the races of Middle-earth sing songs, and the songs they sing reveal vital elements about their cultures"[163]. This can be seen in particular with the former dwarf kingdom that is reconstructed in the song: up to stanza six, the song tells of the former kingdom from the dwarves' present perspective, which is reminiscent of Salman Rushdie's reconstruction of India. In this song, the dwarves create their own imaginary homeland, their 'Erebor of the mind'.

In the first stanza, which is the chorus of the song, the dwarves give a general introduction to and hint at the reason for their mission, while focussing on the location of their home. They are aware that there is a spatial distance between Bilbo's hobbit-hole and their own halls deep within the mountain. In this context, the line "'*Far over the misty mountains cold*'"[164] is important. On the one hand, the Misty Mountains provide a natural border that has to be crossed and which sounds, due to its telling name, dangerous and mysterious. On the other hand, one of the most renowned dwarf kingdoms in Middle-earth had been

---

158 Cf. Corey Olsen. *Exploring* The Hobbit, 29.

159 Amy M. Amendt-Raduege. "'Worthy of a Song': Memory, Mortality and Music.", 114.

160 J.R.R. Tolkien. *The Hobbit*, 17.

161 Cf. Mark Atherton. *There and Back Again*, 60. *An Unexpected Journey*, however, relies on the prose frame narration of Bilbo Baggins rather than on the song to introduce the issue to the viewer; in the movie, the song serves as a means of commemoration, which is a function Amy M. Amendt-Raduege assigns to some of the songs sung in Tolkien's *The Lord of the Rings*. Cf. Amy M. Amendt-Raduege. "'Worthy of a Song': Memory, Mortality and Music.", 114.

162 Cf. Dennis Walder. *Postcolonial Nostalgias*, 6.

163 Amy M. Amendt-Raduege. "'Worthy of a Song': Memory, Mortality and Music.", 118.

164 Appendix: "Song of the Lonely Mountain", l. 1.

situated in the Misty Mountains, Moria. Thus, the adjective "cold" can also be seen in the context of the Balrog's attack. The mines and halls of Moria are no longer inhabited by dwarves and the workshops remain cold and unused.[165] Apart from the Misty Mountains, the dwarves also name the goal of their quest: The "'*dungeons deep and caverns old*'"[166], which stress that "[t]he settings within the song are all dark and ominous, full of subterranean gloom"[167]. Especially the combination of dungeons, as underground prisons, and depth contributes to this impression. At the same time, the age of the caves establishes a connection with underground settings to be found in legends and folklore, and hints at the possibility that these caves may contain a treasure.[168] The feeling of gloom is enhanced, once more, when the dwarves state that they have to leave before the break of day.[169] This might refer to either night or twilight, so that they have the possibility of walking unseen and reinforces the dwarves' preference for darkness.[170]

In addition to that, the fourth and arguably most important line of the chorus refers to "'*pale enchanted gold*'"[171]. While the idea of an enchanted treasure can be found in medieval sources,[172] the attribute "pale" is rather unusual. The

---

165 This idea is also drawn upon in the song Gimli sings about Moria, in which he states that "'*The forge's fire is ashen-cold*'". J.R.R. Tolkien. *The Fellowship of the Ring*, 412.

166 Appendix: "Song of the Lonely Mountain", l. 2.

167 Corey Olsen. *Exploring* The Hobbit, 31.

168 Steve Walker provides yet another interpretation and sees the references in the song as a means of foreshadowing: "The dwarves enlarge the prefiguration potential of those narrative echoes by singing a ballad that simultaneously recalls history and outlines the coming adventure. That historic lay, in its celebration of past events, foreshadows such future incidents as the party's capture by goblins in 'dungeon's deep and caverns old,' escape from wargs through the 'flaming spread' of Gandalf's fire, unleashing of 'the dragon's ire' on Dale, and the 'dying fall' of Thorin in the final battle". Steve Walker. *The Power of Tolkien's Prose*, 79.

169 Cf. Appendix: "Song of the Lonely Mountain", l. 3. It is particularly striking that the German translation (Wolfgang Krege) alters lines three and four in their meaning: "'*Da ziehn wir hin, da lockt Gewinn / An Gold und Silber und Geschmeid*'". The focus has shifted towards the treasure in the mountain, which is seen as a reward for killing the dragon. According to these lines, their quest is neither a matter of urgency nor has to be carried out in secrecy. Douglas A. Anderson. *Das große Hobbit Buch*, 73, original emphasis.

170 Cf. J.R.R. Tolkien. *The Hobbit*, 20. In the appendix to "The Quest of Erebor", in which extracts from an earlier version of the tale are included, Gandalf foregrounds the aspect of secrecy by advising Thorin "'you will have to go on this quest yourself, and you will have to go *secretly*'", which implies that the dwarves may have chosen this time of the day on purpose, as the roads are usually empty. J.R.R. Tolkien. "The Quest of Erebor.", 430, original emphasis.

171 Appendix: "Song of the Lonely Mountain", l. 4.

172 In the Old English epic poem *Beowulf*, for instance, the treasure is enchanted in a way that no one can touch it. Another case in point is 'The Second Lay of Sigurd Fafnicide' of *The Edda of Sæmund the Learned*, in which the dwarf Andvari curses his own treasure.

gold may appear pale because it is simply piled up and stored and no longer in use.[173] At this point in the song, the dwarves do not make a personal claim on the treasure. This claim (in the form of the personal pronoun 'our') is only introduced in the fifth and tenth stanzas, in which the final line of the chorus is altered.[174] Olsen remarks that this personal claim "is important, for at this point [in stanza five] the focus of the song turns from the treasure alone to the dwarves' relationship with it"[175]. This shift of meaning can also be observed in the alterations of "'*pale enchanted gold*'", which is first changed to "'*long-forgotten gold*'"[176] and finally to "'*To win our harps and gold from him*'"[177]. The first alteration in stanza five is significant, because neither the dwarves nor the other peoples have truly forgotten the ancient treasures of Erebor. It even picks up on the idea of the first stanza, in which the treasure is introduced as something mythical and legendary of songs and tales. When considering the gold as a pars pro toto for the entire treasure, the tenth stanza expresses the dwarves' ultimate goal, namely to win back their ancient treasure.[178] The objects used to refer to the treasure are particularly striking, since the gold represents material wealth and heritage, whereas the harps are associated with community and feasting, i.e. tradition. Despite the fact that Mark Atherton claims that "[t]he purpose of the expedition according to Thorin is to recover his inheritance, but according to the song it is to seek 'pale enchanted gold'"[179], the song clearly expands the dwarves' goal from regaining the treasure to recovering dwarf culture, i.e., their kingdom and an old way of life.

In the intermediate stanzas, the idea of diaspora and nostalgic feelings, which entail a glorification of the past, are addressed when the dwarves reconstruct their kingdom in their imagination. In their song, the dwarves state that their ancestors "'*made mighty spells*'"[180], which refers to their ability to create beautiful objects out of the gems and metals they found inside the Lonely Mountain. The reference to spells does not only connect the second stanza with the first by reinforcing the idea of enchantment, but it also makes their creations particularly valuable, since these objects seem to cast spells over men and other peoples. Another instance of idealisation and glorification can be found in the next line,

---

173 This interpretation ties in with the idea that paleness is often connected with death. This connection is, for instance, established in John Keats' ballad "La Belle Dame Sans Merci": in the ballad, the dying knight tells about his last dream, in which he "saw pale kings and Princes too / Pale warriors, death pale were they all", who warn him of the seductive powers of the belle dame and have, apparently, already fallen victim to her. John Keats. "La Belle Dame Sans Merci.", 167, ll. 37-38.

174 Cf. Appendix: "Song of the Lonely Mountain", ll. 20, 40.

175 Corey Olsen. *Exploring* The Hobbit, 31.

176 Appendix: "Song of the Lonely Mountain", l. 20.

177 Ibid., l. 40.

178 Cf. ibid.

179 Mark Atherton. *There and Back Again*, 60.

180 Appendix: "Song of the Lonely Mountain", l. 5.

in which the sound of hammers is compared to that of "'*ringing bells*'"[181]. This image, however, is not overall positive, as it is contrasted with dark things that sleep in the depths,[182] which can be read as a direct reference to the Balrog of Moria. While sleeping is something inactive and passive, the hammering of the dwarves is active and connected with movement. It is the way in which the mountain is transformed by the dwarves, because they move inside and shape the interior of the mountain, that is by mining for gems and metals and by expanding their "'*hollow halls*'"[183], which are referred to at the end of the stanza. This means that the mountain in its outer appearance is still a natural space, while the interior of the mountain is that of a kingdom, hence of culture.

In the following two stanzas, the dwarves indulge in reminiscences of the beautiful objects and skills of their ancestors, which, according to Gerard Hynes, are hardly distinguished in the song.[184] In this context, Atherton even claims that "[s]tanzas three and four speak of a king of the elves in ancient times, who commissioned the dwarvish goldsmiths to produce their masterpieces of finely made silver carcanets – jewelled collars or necklaces"[185]. However, his interpretation of a single commissioner proves to be difficult, because the dwarves hint at both men and elves, who saw the dwarvish treasure as "'*a gleaming golden hoard*'"[186]. Rateliff even claims with regard to these lines that they speak "not just of the dwarves' skill but of the elves' recognition thereof"[187]. His observation implies that the dwarves' skills have been admired by the elves and highlights that they were widely known as skilled craftsmen and were presumably even more skilled than the elves. This idea is highlighted during a conversation between the dwarves and Bilbo, when Balin and Thorin remember the hoard in detail. They think of the spears that were made for King Bladorthin[188], the great golden cup that was forged for their own king Thror and the precious necklace that was made for Girion, the Lord of Dale.[189] Moreover, there is no indication

---

181 Appendix: "Song of the Lonely Mountain", l. 6.

182 Cf. ibid., l. 7.

183 Ibid., l. 8.

184 Cf. Gerard Hynes. "From Nauglath to Durin's Folk.", 22. He exemplifies the close connection between craft and beauty by focusing on Thorin's description of the Arkenstone, which highlights the stone's beauty rather than its value, as well as on Fili and Kili, who think about making music when they see the treasure. Cf. ibid.

185 Mark Atherton. *There and Back Again*, 61.

186 Appendix: "Song of the Lonely Mountain", l. 10. This clearly is an outdated point of view: Thorin and his company see the "'*pale enchanted gold*'" rather than a "'*gleaming golden hoard*'". Ibid., ll. 4, 10.

187 John D. Rateliff. "Anchoring the Myth.", 14.

188 Although Tyler claims that King Bladorthin was a king or ruler of the elves, Robert Foster is more doubtful about his elvish origin. Cf. "Bladorthin." in: J.E.A. Tyler. *The Tolkien Companion*, 66.; cf. "Bladorthin." in: Robert Foster. *A Guide to Middle-Earth*, 33. Tolkien never gave detailed information on King Bladorthin, which is the reason why his origin remains subject to discussion.

189 Cf. J.R.R. Tolkien. *The Hobbit*, 267-68.

in the two stanzas that there is a commissioner for the dwarves' objects. On the contrary, it is rather the dwarves' skills that are emphasised and which make the objects valuable and precious. Furthermore, the fact that the craftsmen were able to shape gems so that they catch the light makes the gems not only beautiful, but also an indication of extremely skilled craftsmen. These objects highlight that "[a]lthough the home of the dwarves sounds dark and gloomy, the works of craft that the dwarves make are, by contrast, associated with light"[190], which is hinted at in the fourth stanza, in which the dwarves state that their ancestors "'*meshed the light of moon and sun*'"[191]. Mark Atherton claims that it "is the magic that the dwarvish goldsmiths used to entrap the light of sun and moon within their artefacts"[192]. Corey Olsen goes beyond this assumption and maintains that "[t]he dwarves apparently do not need the sun in their deep and shadowy halls; their 'gleaming golden hoard' is their sun and moon, the focus of their love and their passion"[193]. This line of the stanza also hints at another, more simple aspect: sunlight is frequently associated with a golden colour and moonlight with a silver colour and draws attention to the materials used in their artefacts and objects.[194] In this respect, a striking connection with the Two Trees of Valinor in Tolkien's *The Silmarillion* can be established, where the connection between golden sunlight and silver moonlight is also used. The two trees, Telperion and Laurelin, were created by the Vala Yavanna and were sources of light, Telperion's light was silver and Laurelin's golden:

> The one had leaves of dark green that beneath were as shining silver, and from each of his countless flowers a dew of silver light was ever falling, and the earth beneath was dappled with the shadows of his fluttering leaves. The other bore leaves of a young green like the new-opened beech; their edges were of glittering gold. Flowers swung upon her branches in clusters of yellow flame, formed each to a glowing horn that spilled a golden rain upon the ground; and from the blossom of that tree there came forth warmth and a great light.[195]

After both trees had been attacked by Melkor and died, Yavanna and Nienna attempted to 'heal' them and eventually a silver bough of Telperion and a golden fruit of Laurelin grew again and were transformed into vessels of the moon and the sun respectively, which highlights their symbolic significance in

---

190 Corey Olsen. *Exploring* The Hobbit, 31.

191 Appendix: "Song of the Lonely Mountain", l. 16.

192 Mark Atherton. *There and Back Again*, 60.

193 Corey Olsen. *Exploring* The Hobbit, 31.

194 This connection is prominently used in fairy tales, as Max Lüthi explains: "But because the beautiful in it [the fairy tale] so often appears as gold or luster, especially as metallic luster, the fairytale takes on the shimmer of the perfect, the indestructible, the timeless, the absolute, and with it that of the transcending, even of the transcendent. Gold has probably always been a symbol of the sun, or at least been connected with the sun". Max Lüthi. *The Fairytale*, 13.

195 J.R.R. Tolkien. *The Silmarillion*, 31.

The Silmarillion.[196] Even before their destruction, Fëanor "pondered how the light of the Trees, *the glory of the Blessed Realm*, might be preserved imperishable"[197] and created the Silmarils, which underlines the strong connection between the trees and the creation of extremely valuable and highly elaborate objects. In a similar vein, the dwarves, as advanced craftsmen, created objects along these lines, such as silver necklaces adorned with "'*flowering stars*'"[198], golden crowns, or even combined both 'sun-' and 'moonlight' in their artefacts.[199]

While the first five stanzas describe the ancient kingdom and the production of the dwarves' famous objects, the sixth stanza centres on the dwarves' tradition and their culture. The artefacts mentioned in this stanza are associated with the semantic fields of music and feasting: the dwarves created goblets and harps of gold, which are connected with community and prosperity and represent the glorious days of the former kingdom. This strong focus on community also finds expression in the medium of the song, which is sung by the dwarves and accompanied by their instruments. Despite planning to embark on a perilous journey, they are not equipped with weapons but with their instruments,[200] which are a sign for the dwarves' craftsmanship that is not only apparent in the instruments, but also in their effect as can be seen when Thorin plays his "beautiful golden harp"[201] and enchants Bilbo Baggins. Further aspects that can be found in this stanza are a strong focus on the dwarves' remote habitat and the items they forged for themselves that led Corey Olsen to conclude that this stanza hints at the dwarves' "secrecy and possessiveness"[202]. Similar to the secrecy revolving around their language, the dwarves stress the idea of remaining among themselves by references such as "'*where no man delves*'"[203] or "'*[w]as sung un-*

---

196 Cf. J.R.R. Tolkien. *The Silmarillion*, 109. These vessels, however, could not move on their own accord, which is why they were guided by two Maiar: "The maiden whom the Valar chose from among the Maiar to guide the vessel of the Sun was named Arien, and he that steered the island of the Moon was Tilion". Ibid., 110.

197 Ibid., 68, my emphasis.

198 Appendix: "Song of the Lonely Mountain", l. 14. The idea of starlight caught in gems is picked up in Peter Jackson's *The Desolation of Smaug*: the elf-king Thranduil, who apparently has a claim on these stones, says that "'[t]here are gems in the mountain that I too desire. White gems of pure starlight'". Peter Jackson. *The Desolation of Smaug*, 00:37:05-00:37:12. In *The Battle of the Five Armies*, Thorin lifts up a necklace made of these gems and identifies them as "'The White Gems of Lasgalen'"; in this context, he also indirectly refers to Thranduil, which reinforces that these are the stones the elf-king referred to beforehand. Peter Jackson. *The Battle of the Five Armies*, 00:41:04-00:41:13.

199 Cf. Appendix: "Song of the Lonely Mountain", ll. 13-16.

200 These instruments include fiddles, flutes, a drum, clarinets, viols and a harp. Cf. J.R.R. Tolkien. *The Hobbit*, 17.

201 J.R.R. Tolkien. *The Hobbit*, 17.

202 Corey Olsen. *Exploring* The Hobbit, 32.

203 Appendix: "Song of the Lonely Mountain", l. 22.

heard by men or elves'"[204]. This is also a topic that is addressed in Peter Jackson's adaptation, in which Thorin initially does not fully acknowledge Bilbo as a part of the company.[205]

Up until this point, the song is used by the dwarves to conjure up their lost kingdom and expresses their own view of their past and their former home.[206] The first part of this song suggests that the dwarves' notion of home is that to be found in the 'Odyssean pattern' as identified by Lucy Waddey, because the dwarves "romanticize their [...] [home]"[207]. The memory of their ancient kingdom does not only evoke the feeling of nostalgia, but also highlights the dwarves' determination to reclaim their home; arguably they are living hope and loss at the same time.[208] The dwarves have lost a kingdom that is connected with a specific location, their ancestors as well as with community and their own culture and they still hope to restore the kingdom of old. In appendix A to *The Lord of the Rings*, this hope is, for instance, expressed in Thorin's answer to Thrain's question whether he would like to go back to the anvil or "'beg [...] [his] bread at proud doors?'". Thorin responds: "'To the anvil [...]. The hammer will at least keep the arms strong, until they can wield sharper tools *again*'"[209]. In saying this, Thorin hints at the fact that, while living in his present state as a diasporic and dispossessed dwarf, he is "remembering/desiring another place"[210], where he can use his full potential again. In *The Hobbit*, a different expression of hope for the restoration of the kingdom can be found in Lake-town: while some of the inhabitants clearly deny the existence of a King under the Mountain, others burst into songs about the return of the dwarf king, because the people of Lake-town hope that upon the king's return "gold [...] [will] flow in rivers, through the mountain-gates" and "all that land [...] [will] be filled with new song and new laughter".[211] One of their songs is listed by Tolkien and tells

---

[204] Appendix: "Song of the Lonely Mountain", l. 24. Gerard Hynes also analyses this line of the song and argues that "[t]he song also emphasizes that dwarves have a culture and a tradition of art of which humans and elves are entirely ignorant", which demonstrates that it might also hint at the relationship between dwarves, elves and humans. Gerard Hynes. "From Nauglath to Durin's Folk.", 25.

[205] This can be seen, for instance, in the discussion between Bilbo and Bofur in the entrance to the goblin's cave, when Bofur says: "'No, no, you can't turn back now, eh? You're part of the company. You're one of us'" and Bilbo responds: "'I'm not, though, am I? Thorin said I should never have come and he was right'". Peter Jackson. *An Unexpected Journey*, 01:46:39-01:46:49. This is likewise apparent in Thorin's choice of words when speaking about Bilbo, to whom he often refers as 'the burglar'.

[206] This idea was also picked up in the song by Neil Finn that is played during the credits of Jackson's *An Unexpected Journey*, in which he sings that the dwarves have "for home a song that echoes on". Ibid., 02:36:08-02:36:10.

[207] Lucy Waddey. "Home in Children's Literature.", 13.

[208] Cf. James Clifford. "Diasporas.", 454.

[209] J.R.R. Tolkien. *The Return of the King*, 1413, my emphasis.

[210] James Clifford. "Diasporas.", 453.

[211] J.R.R. Tolkien. *The Hobbit*, 222.

of the legendary return of the dwarves and the effect on the landscape: "'*The woods shall wave on mountains / And grass beneath the sun; / His wealth shall flow in fountains / And the rivers golden run. / The streams shall run in gladness, / The lakes shall shine and burn, / All sorrow fail and sadness / At the Mountain-king's return!*'"[212]. This song serves the purpose of giving the dwarf company new hope, i.e. it functions as an additional stimulus. It is, to put it in Corey Olsen's words, "[u]nder the influence of enthusiastic songs in Lake-town, [that] they have been swept up into thinking about the re-establishment of the fabled dwarvish Kingdom Under the Mountain"[213]. However, the place the dwarves hope to find is the one they sang about in the 'Song of the Lonely Mountain', it is their own version of Erebor that is recollected from the fragments of their memories. In the context of home and the feeling of nostalgia, Nicole Schröder assesses that

> home is central to human life and maybe nostalgia is one significant part of the notion of home. Yet I would argue that such nostalgia and idealization are also dangerous as they threaten to locate home somewhere in the past and turn it into an ideal place that can never again be reached.[214]

Even though the dwarves may reclaim the mountain, they have to establish their own kingdom. The kingdom in the 'Song of the Lonely Mountain' does no longer exist and a reproduction can only become an approximation.

2.3 Harps, Gems and Gold: The Treasure in Erebor

When Bilbo Baggins explains to Smaug "'[n]ot gold alone brought us hither'"[215], he points out that the dwarves hope to recover more than the huge amount of gold stored in the mountain – but the treasure is among the chief motivations to regain Erebor. This treasure consists of gold, harps and other musical instruments, precious gems and crowns, to name just a few of the items to be found in the mountain. The range of different objects can, for instance, be seen in the recollection of the treasure by Balin and Thorin after Bilbo faced the dragon for the first time and successfully returned:

> From that the talk turned to the great hoard itself and to the things that Thorin and Balin remembered. They wondered if they were still lying there unharmed in the hall below: the spears that were made for the armies of the great King Bladorthin (long since dead), each had a thrice-forged head and their shafts were inlaid with cunning gold, but they were never delivered or paid for; shields made for warriors long dead; the great golden cup of Thror, two-handed, hammered and carven with birds and flowers whose eyes and petals were of jewels; coats of mail gilded and silvered and impenetrable; the necklace of Girion,

212 J.R.R. Tolkien. *The Hobbit*, 230, original emphasis.
213 Corey Olsen. *Exploring* The Hobbit, 196.
214 Nicole Schröder. *Spaces and Places in Motion*, 35.
215 J.R.R. Tolkien. *The Hobbit*, 260.

> Lord of Dale, made of five hundred emeralds green as grass, which he gave for the arming of his eldest son in a coat of dwarf-linked rings the like of which had never been made before, for it was wrought of pure silver to the power and strength of triple steel. But fairest of all was the great white gem, which the dwarves had found beneath the roots of the Mountain, the Heart of the Mountain, the Arkenstone of Thrain.[216]

This recollection gives a more detailed description of individual objects that are particularly well remembered by Balin and Thorin, not least because of their relevance for and connection to the great kings and lords for whom they were created. These items range from war equipment (spears, shields and coats of mail) and objects associated with feasting (the golden cup) to jewellery and gemstones (Girion's necklace and the Arkenstone). The emphasis on war equipment is striking in this account, because the 'Song of the Lonely Mountain' predominantly addressed jewellery – war equipment was only mentioned in passing, for example by the reference to the "'*hilt of sword*'"[217] that was adorned with gems. The reference to weapons and armour adds two layers of interpretation: firstly, the spears, shields and coats of mail have special properties that were inlaid by the dwarves and confirm their skills, which can, for instance, be seen in the coat of mail that makes its bearer invulnerable.[218] Secondly, these items belong to the past, since the armies and warriors for whom the items have been made are "long dead".[219] At this point, Thorin and Balin become aware that although they might have bridged the spatial distance to their home, the temporal gap remains;[220] this does not diminish their desire for these objects, however. With the other items, the focus lies on their appearance and the valuable materials that have been used to craft them, such as the emeralds in Girion's necklace or the number of jewels adorning Thror's cup.

In their enumeration Balin and Thorin also introduce the most precious and most unique object of the whole hoard, namely the Arkenstone of Thrain. Al-

216 J.R.R. Tolkien. *The Hobbit*, 267-68.

217 Appendix: "Song of the Lonely Mountain", l. 12.

218 It can be assumed that these coats were made of mithril, the precious metal the dwarves mined in Moria. This idea is reinforced by the mithril coat that Bilbo receives from Thorin when they explore the dragon's hoard. Cf. J.R.R. Tolkien. *The Hobbit*, 277-78. In Peter Jackson's adaptation, Thorin stresses the protective powers associated with mithril coats: "'This vest is made of silver steel. Mithril it was called by my forebears. *No blade can pierce it*'". Peter Jackson. *The Battle of the Five Armies*, 00:47:27-00:47:42, my emphasis.

219 At a later point in the story, the link between the treasure and the memories of the old days is made explicit: "Long hours in the past days Thorin had spent in the treasury, and the lust of it was heavy on him. Though he had hunted chiefly for the Arkenstone, yet he had an eye for many other wonderful thing that was lying there, *about which were wound old memories of the labours and the sorrows of his race*". J.R.R. Tolkien. *The Hobbit*, 306, my emphasis.

220 This idea is reminiscent of Rushdie's experiences in India. Cf. Salman Rushdie. "Imaginary Homelands.", 9-10.

though this jewel is priceless for Thorin, it is generally considered to be "'worth more than a river of gold'"[221], and, as Thorin accentuates in the movie adaptation, the reason why Bilbo is with them.[222] In his analysis of this "great white gem of brilliant translucency"[223], Mark Atherton analyses the Arkenstone's meaning in comparison with the One Ring in *The Lord of the Rings* and the Silmarils in *The Silmarillion.*[224] He claims that similar to the Silmarils, the Arkenstone "is a source of enchantment, the focus of men's desires and self-interests, a symbol of power in the political games that the various peoples of the story have to play"[225]. The focus on (dwarvish) desire and self-interest can be observed with Thorin, to whom the Arkenstone is not only the most important item of the whole hoard, but also part of his family's inheritance and his object of desire. Its connection with power is indicated more strongly in Peter Jackson's audio-visual adaptation, in which the Arkenstone is also named 'The King's Jewel' and linked with rulership, because Thror takes the Arkenstone as "'a sign that his right to rule was divine'"[226].

But Atherton also hints at the vital difference between the Arkenstone, the One Ring and the Silmarils, even though they share several similarities. He assumes that "[t]he rule is that the artisan or maker invests the artefact he has made with his desires, will and emotions"[227]. While this proves to be true for the One Ring, which "is bound up with the lust for power that has been projected into it by its architect and artisan Sauron"[228], and the Silmarils, which "are bound up with the personality of their maker Fëanor and his descendants"[229], it proves to be different for the Arkenstone. Thorin describes the Arkenstone as follows: "'The Arkenstone! The Arkenstone! [...] It was like a globe with a thousand facets; it shone like silver in the firelight, like water in the sun, like snow under the stars, like rain upon the Moon!'"[230]. While the Silmarils and the One Ring are made by an artisan, as Atherton notes, "[t]he imagery [connected with the Arkenstone] all derives from natural phenomena: fire, water, snow and rain; and this is the crux: the Arkenstone is a natural phenomenon"[231]. But his

221 J.R.R. Tolkien. *The Hobbit*, 309.

222 Cf. Peter Jackson. *The Desolation of Smaug*, 01:39:34-01:39:39.

223 "Arkenstone." in: J.E.A. Tyler. *The Tolkien Companion*, 25.

224 Cf. Mark Atherton. *There and Back Again*, 73-75. In *The History of the Hobbit*, John D. Rateliff also includes a subchapter on "The Arkenstone as Silmaril", in which he has a closer look at the origins of the Arkenstone in Tolkien's legendarium and even speculates whether the Arkenstone is one of the three Silmarils created by Fëanor. Cf. John D. Rateliff. *The History of The Hobbit*, 603-609.

225 Mark Atherton. *There and Back Again*, 73.

226 Peter Jackson. *An Unexpected Journey*, 00:03:33-00:03:36.

227 Mark Atherton. *There and Back Again*, 73.

228 Ibid., 74.

229 Ibid.

230 J.R.R. Tolkien. *The Hobbit*, 268.

231 Mark Atherton. *There and Back Again*, 74.

statement can also be expanded, since Thorin's comparisons are not only natural phenomena, but they are almost exclusively those of water and light. The mixture of these natural phenomena ultimately leads to the Arkenstone's appearance in rainbow colours, as can be seen when Bilbo finds the gemstone, which "was tinged with a flickering sparkle of many colours at the surface, reflected and splintered from the wavering light of his torch"[232]. In addition to that, the Arkenstone seems to be the epitome of what the dwarves have sung about in the 'Song of the Lonely Mountain'. While the dwarves usually set the gemstones in a way to make them reflect the light, the Arkenstone does not need an external source of light but radiates light of its own accord.[233] This curious property is, according to Olsen, the reason why Thorin is overcome with the desire for the precious gemstone: "Thorin's love for the Arkenstone is not a reflection of his reverence for the craftsmanship of his forefathers; it is a love for a beauty and wonder outside and beyond the skill of the dwarves, discovered by them at the roots of the Mountain"[234]. However, the 'Heart of the Mountain' is no longer an entirely natural gemstone, since the dwarves "cut and fashioned"[235] it, so that Olsen's comment can only be partly applied to the Arkenstone.

The Arkenstone's alternative name 'Heart of the Mountain' is extraordinary and permits the assumption that "to a certain extent the Mountain is also imbued with personality"[236]. When the company is on their way to Lake-town and approaches the Lonely Mountain, it has "its dark head in a torn cloud"[237] and seems "to frown at him [Bilbo] and threaten him as it drew ever nearer"[238]. These references reinforce that

> [i]n Tolkien's fiction, especially perhaps in his tales of Middle-earth, nature is an animate presence. Middle-earth is much more than a backdrop against which a plot is played out: it is awake and sentient. Natural elements and features are given character, agency, and even personality.[239]

---

232 J.R.R. Tolkien. *The Hobbit*, 274.

233 This assumption is further consolidated by the description of the stone when Bilbo hands it over to Bard: "It was as if a globe had been filled with moonlight and hung before them in a net woven of the glint of frosty stars". Ibid., 314.

234 Corey Olsen. *Exploring* The Hobbit, 235. By contrast, Frank P. Riga, Maureen Thum and Judith Kollmann assume that in Peter Jackson's adaptations "Thorin is obsessed with the Arkenstone, not necessarily for its value and beauty, although these may be factors, but because of its symbolic value". Frank P. Riga, Maureen Thum and Judith Kollmann. "From Children's Book to Epic Prequel.", 113-14.

235 J.R.R. Tolkien. *The Hobbit*, 274.

236 Mark Atherton. *There and Back Again*, 74.

237 J.R.R. Tolkien. *The Hobbit*, 219.

238 Ibid., 221.

239 Liam Campbell. "Nature.", 440.

The mountain's 'face' and its roots clearly hint at the fact that the mountain is an animate being.[240] Peter Jackson suggests this animate nature of the mountain even more strongly by elaborating on the 'body metaphor'. This metaphor is visualised in the mountain's interior walls, which are crossed by veins of gold.[241] Assuming an animate nature of the mountain, the dwarves sealed their own fate and doom by literally taking the 'Heart of the Mountain'. Although more than seven centuries pass between the foundation of the dwarf kingdom (T.A. (Third Age) 1999) and its destruction by Smaug (T.A. 2770), the adaptation suggests that the dragon's attack took place only shortly afterwards. Thus it seems that the mountain is unable to live on without its heart and that the taking of the Arkenstone resulted in the dragon's attack. In both the novel and the movie the dragon is then, just like the Balrog in Moria, seen as a punishment for the greed and avarice of the dwarves, who delved into and found the Arkenstone "*beneath* the roots of the Mountain"[242], but the film highlights this link even more.

An important issue that is connected with greed is 'dragon-sickness', the love for gold that resulted in the destruction of Erebor. It seems as if the dwarves' own "'*mighty spells*'"[243] have backfired, because Thror, even more than Thorin, became obsessed with a love for gold and jewels.[244] Michael N. Stanton indicates that this form of greed is "the motive for the return of Balin and others [...] in spite of these known dangers [the dragon]"[245]. Interestingly, he names Balin

---

240 Cf. Mark Atherton. *There and Back Again*, 75. In his analysis of the hoard, Atherton notes that Bilbo is often 'drawn' to the treasure; he argues that "[t]he past participle *drawn* is agentive in the sense that it implies an *agent* – someone or something is drawing him towards it" and uses Bilbo's finding of the Arkenstone as one of his examples. Ibid., 71, original emphasis. Paul Acker, Matthews Bardowell and Jeffrey Weinstock remark that it is presumably this jewel (along with the other treasure) that allured the dragon to conquer the mountain, which supports Atherton's assumption. Cf. Paul Acker, Matthew Bardowell and Jeffrey A. Weinstock. "Dwarf.", 200.

241 Despite the fact that Bilbo's voice-over describes them as "'seams of gold'", their depiction resembles veins rather than seams. Peter Jackson. *An Unexpected Journey*, 00:02:52. Two scenes in Jackson's *An Unexpected Journey* illustrate this: firstly, the 'throne room', in which a huge stalactite crossed by golden veins connects the ceiling and Thror's throne. Secondly, when the miners, who are digging for gold, are shown, several of the veins of gold in the depths of the mountain are revealed. Cf. ibid., 00:02:27; 00:02:56.

242 J.R.R. Tolkien. *The Hobbit*, 268, my emphasis. The location of the object of Smaug's and the Balrog's desire is similar, the mithril-lode can be found near the roots of Barazinbar (Caradhras) and the Arkenstone rests beneath the roots of the Lonely Mountain. Both objects are situated in subterranean depths and are discovered by greedily mining dwarves.

243 Appendix: "Song of the Lonely Mountain", l. 5.

244 The narrator in *The Hobbit* even remarks that this love for gold and jewels can be found in all dwarves: "and when the heart of a dwarf, even the most respectable, is wakened by gold and by jewels, he grows suddenly bold, and he may become fierce". J.R.R. Tolkien. *The Hobbit*, 276-77.

245 Michael N. Stanton. *Hobbits, Elves, and Wizards*, 109.

and not Thorin, whose desire centres around a single object, the Arkenstone, while the other dwarves value quantity over quality, as can be seen when "they gathered gems and stuffed their pockets, and let what they could not carry fall back through their fingers with a sigh"[246]. Film critic Kate Muir goes a step further and observes with focus on Peter Jackson's adaptations that Thorin "becomes crazed by the 'dragon sickness', an ugly greed *that pervades the place* [Erebor]"[247]. Her statement implies that the destination of the dwarves' journey is simultaneously a source of doom and decay. Thus, Erebor becomes the epitome of illness and demise rather than a place connected to life and prosperity, which reinforces the ambivalent nature of the mountain.

When the dwarves sang the 'Song of the Lonely Mountain' at Bag-End, Bilbo created Erebor in his mind. However, the actual 'encounter' with the mountain and the treasure is very different from what the hobbit imagined. The dwarves have already lived in this place and associate it with notions of home, wealth and glorious reigns, whereas the hobbit was only mentally 'relocated' during the song and developed his own version of Erebor, including thoughts about the size and appearance of the treasure. This mental creation turns into a 'lived' place when he sees the treasure and walks on the hoard for the very first time. Although he is aware that this is the place the dwarves sang about in their song, it appears to be different from what he has imagined. He accuses the dwarves: "'you cannot pretend that you ever made the vast extent of his [Thorin's grandfather's] wealth clear to me'"[248]. The formerly varying perspectives on the treasure are conflated by the treasure's actual manifestation. The closer the dwarves get to the mountain and to their treasure, the more information Bilbo receives on its actual nature, through which he is able to connect and adjust his former ideas of Erebor. Even after the dwarves have once more access to their treasure, they are – similar to Rushdie's experiences in India – not "capable of reclaiming precisely the thing that was lost"[249]. They may be able to "'*win our harps and gold*'"[250] from the dragon, as the 'Song of the Lonely Mountain' predicted, but they have to create their own kingdom, which might be based on the former appearance and glory of Erebor.

2.4 Peter Jackson's Visual Creation of Erebor

Apart from the depictions in the novel and the drawing 'Conversation with Smaug'[251], Tolkien gives hardly any information on the interior of Erebor. This lack evokes the impression that his dwarves are primarily concerned with the

246 J.R.R. Tolkien. *The Hobbit*, 277.

247 Kate Muir. "One Film to End Them All.", n.p., my emphasis.

248 J.R.R. Tolkien. *The Hobbit*, 255.

249 Salman Rushdie. "Imaginary Homelands.", 10.

250 Appendix: "Song of the Lonely Mountain", l. 40.

251 Douglas A. Anderson. *Das große Hobbit Buch*, n.p.

treasure and the kingdom as a whole, so that their view largely ignores the interior appearance of the Lonely Mountain. Peter Jackson, by contrast, needed to visually elaborate on the interior parts prior to their destruction by the rampaging dragon. He expands Tolkien's novel "by not only completing the work, but also by translating the work of art from one medium to another, from children's novel to adult film"[252] and in the process makes several changes.

Unlike Tolkien's novel, Jackson's adaptation gives considerable recognition to the dwarf kingdom of old, especially in the frame narrative of the old Bilbo Baggins. This shift in narrative position and the change in medium have several consequences, which contribute to the creation and perception of Erebor in the audio-visual adaptations. The first movie does not solely rely on Thorin's description of the events but chooses Bilbo as narrator for an event he could never have witnessed, since the temporal gap between the dragon's attack (T.A. 2770) and his birth in the Shire (T.A. 2890) amounts to 120 years.[253] Using Bilbo as a narrator in the movie is, however, not a far-fetched choice, because he is the main focalizer in Tolkien's novel. At the beginning of *The Hobbit*, the protagonist is not yet familiar with the dwarves and their quest and lacks knowledge about Erebor. Throughout the story, he is "sharing their [the dwarves'] experiences but not their perspective"[254] regarding both the former dwarf kingdom and the reasons for their quest. While Bilbo receives most of the information on Erebor and the Arkenstone only gradually, the viewer of *An Unexpected Journey* is provided with the essential information at the beginning. Within the first four minutes of the movie, the viewer is introduced to the Arkenstone and its function as well as its symbolic meaning in the dwarf kingdom, whereas Bilbo and the reader do not know about the Arkenstone until chapter 12. Consequently, the frame narration in the movie already anticipates the quest plot of the story and addresses the dwarves' goal. By implication, the 'Song of the Lonely Mountain' also shifts in significance, as it does no longer serve primarily as the means to introduce Bilbo to the former dwarf kingdom. The song is shortened in the movie and predominantly serves to express the dwarves' nostalgia and is likely to have a powerful emotional impact on the audience. This impression is achieved by the absence of instruments as well as the fact that some of the dwarves hum and others gradually join in the song. The melancholic atmosphere evoked by and accompanying the song emphasises the importance the dwarves assign to this quest on an emotional level. Thus, from the beginning of the movie, the viewer is introduced to the dwarves' diasporic situation, their determination to regain and reclaim Erebor from the dragon as well as the historical events that precede the actual story. Bilbo's frame narration, which, in terms of its function, is an equivalent of Thorin's account of the events in the novel,

[252] Frank P. Riga, Maureen Thum and Judith Kollmann. "From Children's Book to Epic Prequel.", 98.

[253] Cf. J.R.R. Tolkien. *The Return of the King*, 1428-29.

[254] Corey Olsen. *Exploring* The Hobbit, 232.

facilitates an understanding of the dwarves' situation and contextualises the quest that is to follow.

Jackson's introduction to the dwarf kingdom departs in yet another striking way from the introduction given in the 'Song of the Lonely Mountain' and Thorin's subsequent explanation, namely in its order of settings. The city of Dale, which is shown before the viewers see the dwarf kingdom, is situated at the doors of Erebor; it is referred to as a "'merry town'"[255] with a toy market, which "'was the wonder of the North'"[256]. Due to the fact that Dale is considered a peaceful and affluent city,[257] the relationship between dwarves and men appears to be based on mutual prosperity. This is reinforced by a scene that shows a busy marketplace in Dale where men and dwarves (which can be distinguished from one another by their size and hairstyles) live peacefully alongside one another and trade items.[258] In the background, children enjoy rides on a small merry-go-round and the entire scene is crowded with people who are cheerfully engrossed in conversations.[259] Both the merry-go-round, which hints at "'the most marvellous and magical toys'"[260] the dwarves created, and the jewellery, which is sold by the (presumably) dwarvish lady,[261] indicate trade and prosperity. The introduction to a thriving city serves the purpose of making Erebor appear even more wealthy and splendid. At the same time, the devastation of the city is used to emphasise the destructive powers of the dragon, because it is put to much more effect in the open.

Similar to the stanzas of the 'Song of the Lonely Mountain', which become more detailed with each stanza, the camera zooms from the exterior of Erebor to its interior. Thus, the dwarf kingdom is introduced by showing the front of the 'fortress' and its gate.[262] The greenish colour of the front resembles the walls of

---

255 J.R.R. Tolkien. *The Hobbit*, 28.

256 Ibid.

257 Cf. Peter Jackson. *An Unexpected Journey*, 00:02:00-00:02:03.

258 Cf. ibid., 00:02:05.

259 Cf. ibid.

260 J.R.R. Tolkien. *The Hobbit*, 28.

261 In appendix A to the *Lord of the Rings*, the narrator explains (based on what Gimli said) that dwarf women "seldom walk abroad except at great need" and on journeys they are "so like dwarf-men that the eyes and ears of other peoples cannot tell them apart". J.R.R. Tolkien. *The Return of the King*, 1417. The fact that the woman in Dale is a dwarf woman becomes apparent in her size, because she is smaller by a head than all other women; she shares the dwarves' corpulence and wears an apparently characteristic dwarvish hair style, which is reminiscent of Nori's.

262 Cf. Peter Jackson. *An Unexpected Journey*, 00:02:16. The scene shows the front of Erebor that is part of the mountain wall. While the front is similar in colour to the mountain, the actual gate is set apart by its golden colour and is relatively small in comparison to the entire front. Two huge dwarf statues frame the front gate on both sides and mark the place as the entrance to a dwarf dwelling in the mountains. Apart from that, a small path leads to the gate that is presumably used as a road for trade and as the way to the en-

the mountain, which may be a hint at the dwarves' secretiveness. The front is, however, simultaneously set apart by its size, and the huge dwarf statues next to the gate serve the purpose of representing the folk that lives inside the mountain. They are solid and massive, presumably made of stone or steel (or any other metal) and are indicative of the dwarves' craft.[263] By being depicted in full armour and with levied axes, which generally serve the purpose of intimidating those standing in front of them and to scare away their enemies, the dwarves' militant nature is emphasised.[264] This assumption is enhanced by King Thror's first appearance when he walks on the railing of his 'fortress' past his soldiers; this introduction stresses the impression that his "'[s]tronghold'"[265], as it is called in the movie, is secure and invulnerable. This aspect is also reflected by the choice of words used in Bilbo's voice-over: Erebor is not only referred to as "'the greatest kingdom in Middle-earth'"[266], but it is also ruled by the "'[m]ightiest of the Dwarf Lords'"[267]. The striking uses of the superlative indicate that Erebor exceeds all other kingdoms.

The glory of the kingdom is further drawn upon in the interior of Erebor. For instance, Thror's throne room is lined with huge statues of soldiers, each of them equipped with an axe.[268] In contrast to their counterparts in front of the gate, the statues inside appear to be larger, are ornamented with gold and are used to display the dwarves' skill. Their position on the wall, as part of the columns in the architectural design of the hall, suggests that the dwarves are the 'pillars' on which the kingdom has been built. Apart from the huge statues, the massive stalactite, crossed by golden 'veins', that protrudes from the ceiling and merges with Thror's throne is another element that reinforces this impression. It suggests that the gold is 'flowing' from the mountain directly to the throne and may be seen as a first hint at Thror's avarice. In this context, the position of the throne is crucial: it indicates that the King is in the highest position, physically as well as in the hierarchy, because his kingdom has been built in the depths of

---

trance of the kingdom. The natural environment surrounding the mountain adds to its perception as a harmonious, thriving and peaceful area.

263 Peter Jackson tends to use materials that are associated with the different peoples of Middle-earth to build their homes. For instance, the realm of the wood-elf king is introduced by columns that seem to be made of roots, while the interior of his palace is not only held in brown colours, but also uses wood and roots to a considerable extent. Cf. Peter Jackson. *The Desolation of Smaug*, 00:34:19-00:34:54.

264 Despite the fact that the overall introduction of the dwarves frequently depicts them as soldiers, Balin reminds Thorin after they gave Bilbo the contract: "'It appears we have lost our burglar. Probably for the best. The odds were always against us. After all, what are we? Merchants, miners, tinkers, toy-makers. Heh, heh. Hardly the stuff of legend'". Peter Jackson. *An Unexpected Journey*, 00:32:23-00:32:41.

265 Peter Jackson. *An Unexpected Journey*, 00:02:17.

266 Ibid., 00:02:09-00:02:13.

267 Ibid., 00:02:21-00:02:23.

268 Cf. ibid., 00:02:27.

the mountain.[269] The throne's position implies that the King is sitting on all the riches that accumulate underneath him. Thus, he is, similar to the dragon, 'sitting' on the hoard and treasures of Erebor. Thror's love for gold is made even more explicit in his clothes, which are ornamented with gold applications. In comparison to his son, he wears substantially more gold, while his grandson Thorin "wears a tunic of midnight blue, studded with silver and a large silver belt buckle with a sword at his side"[270], which permits the conclusion that he is least affected by the enchanting influence of the treasure.[271]

Moreover, the interior mountain walls display a colour symbolism that is highlighted by Bilbo's voice-over when he states that the dwarves "'fashion[ed] objects of great beauty out of diamond, emerald, ruby and sapphire'"[272]. Taking the colours in which the gemstones most frequently appear in nature, the blue sapphire, the green emerald and the red ruby are represented in the mountain's walls, which are a mixture of green and blue traversed by red and ornamented with gold. These precious gemstones, in combination with the marble structure of the wall, add to the majestic and simultaneously artificial appearance of the interior of the mountain. Although Tolkien did not describe the pattern and texture of Erebor's walls, his drawing 'Conversation with Smaug'[273] displays a rather natural environment with grey mountain walls, from which Jackson clearly deviates in his own interpretation and depiction of Erebor. Arguably, the dwarf kingdom in Peter Jackson's adaptation is reminiscent of what Dorothy sees when she arrives in the Emerald City in L. Frank Baum's *The Wonderful Wizard of Oz*:

> Even with eyes protected by the green spectacles Dorothy and her friends were at first dazzled by the brilliancy of the wonderful City. The streets were lined with beautiful houses all built of green marble and studded everywhere with sparkling emeralds. They walked

269 The Arkenstone, however, is positioned even higher. Its significance is stressed when the dwarves discover the secret door that leads into Erebor and see a plate indicating that the Arkenstone is at the heart of the kingdom. Cf. Peter Jackson. *The Desolation of Smaug*, 01:39:03.

270 Frank P. Riga, Maureen Thum and Judith Kollmann. "From Children's Book to Epic Prequel.", 113.

271 While Thorin's clothes hardly display any golden ornaments in *An Unexpected Journey*, these feature quite strikingly in *The Battle of the Five Armies*. In the final instalment, he wears his grandfather's crown, which is gold and silver coloured, and a suit of armour with golden applications. The change of his clothes already hints at Thorin's dragon-sickness and his avarice. In this context, he also begins to refer to himself as 'King' and considers the Arkenstone more important than his own kin. As soon as Thorin becomes aware of the influence of the treasure on him, he swaps his armour for a plain coat of mail. Cf. Peter Jackson. *The Battle of the Five Armies*, 01:20:57-01:22:30.

272 Peter Jackson. *An Unexpected Journey*, 00:03:02-00:03:09.

273 Douglas A. Anderson. *Das große Hobbit Buch*, n.p. In the illustration, the treasure room looks rather like a cave or lair than an elaborate and perfectly crafted hall of dwarvish craft.

over a pavement of the same green marble, and where the blocks were joined together were rows of emeralds, set closely, and glittering in the brightness of the sun.[274]

The effect on the viewer of Jackson's *Hobbit* trilogy and in particular the first introduction of Erebor is similar to Dorothy's first impression of the Emerald City, which is likewise associated with wealth and prosperity. As in Baum's city, in which even the pavement consists of marble, the stairs of the dwarf kingdom are made of the same material and the lighting (in the form of torches) accentuates the marble structure of the walls.[275]

In the audio-visual adaptations, the dwarf kingdom is depicted as a huge city that has been built within the mountain. Into the mountain, the dwarves have carved the "'*hollow halls beneath the fells*'"[276] that are mentioned in the 'Song of the Lonely Mountain'. They transformed the place by building houses and workshops. In Bilbo's voice-over even the bell-like hammering that was referred to in the song has been picked up, so that the song can definitely be regarded as one of Jackson's inspirations. Despite the fact that the kingdom appears as a huge city within the mountain, it does not adopt the novel's emphasis on community and comradeship. The depiction of the old kingdom lacks the songs that were "'*sung unheard by men or elves*'"[277]. Instead, the focus is on the depiction of a powerful and mighty city that is connected with the treasure and infused with dragon-sickness.

---

274 L. Frank Baum. *The Wonderful Wizard of Oz*, 175. However, at a later point in the story, the titular wizard reveals the green colour to be a deception: "'But isn't everything here green?' asked Dorothy. 'No more than in any other city,' replied Oz; 'but when you wear green spectacles, why of course everything you see looks green to you. The Emerald City was built a great many years ago, for I was a young man when the balloon brought me here, and I am a very old man now. But my people have worn green glasses on their eyes so long that most of them think it really is an Emerald City, and it certainly is a beautiful place, abounding in jewels and precious metals, and every good thing that is needed to make one happy'". Ibid., 266-68.

275 Using precious metals in cities is, as Max Lüthi observes, also characteristic of those fairy tales that elaborate on the setting: "[a] city or a bridge [...] of metal – whether it is of brass, copper, silver, or gold – is [...] not a curiosity but rather, with its abstract uniformity and timelessness, in its way a perfect creation". Max Lüthi. *The Fairytale*, 20. Arguably, the marble city in the Lonely Mountain conveys the impression of perfection and the dwarves' skill by foregrounding the materials that have been used to build it.

276 Appendix: "Song of the Lonely Mountain", l. 8.

277 Ibid., l. 24.

Part III: The Dragon's Hoard

3.1 A Brief Introduction to Tolkien's Dragons

Even though dragons have never existed, they occupy the minds and thoughts of human beings and are as prevalent in literature as ever. In European folklore, these mythological creatures are considered to be huge fire-breathing monsters that guard hoards of treasure, whereas their Chinese equivalents are linked with more positive attributes and characteristics.[278] David Leeming defines the dragon as follows:

> The dragon is common to many mythological traditions and is usually a giant reptilian creature who spouts fire and steam. [...] In the West the dragon has usually been a symbol of evil against whom heroes such as Sigurd (Siegfried) and Beowulf fight. [...] Dragons often protect treasure, perhaps representing the value of deep understanding to be found in the chthonic depths with which the dragon is also frequently associated.[279]

His definition shows that a dragon's distinctive traits, which are derived from mythology, have been retained. These traits include aspects such as guarding a treasure, breathing fire or the association with evil. But the connotations attached to the word 'dragon' are not restricted to the dragon's characteristics and habits – they also include their dark and dangerous habitat, as well as their role as frightening antagonists. Sandra Unerman notes that dragons "live on in popular culture and in fiction, not as a static symbol but as images which may be used in different ways and given different functions"[280]. Among her examples, she briefly refers to J.K. Rowling's *Harry Potter* series and the baby dragon Norbert in *Harry Potter and the Philosopher's Stone* (1997).[281] Despite Hagrid's attempts at keeping the newly hatched dragon as a pet, Norbert eventually "causes so much trouble [that] he agrees to send it away"[282]. The baby dragon is a good example to illustrate different images of dragons; this is aptly captured in Ron's remark, who explains to Harry and Hermione after having been bitten by the dragon: "'I tell you, that dragon's the most horrible animal I've ever met, but the way Hagrid goes on about it, you'd think it was a fluffy little bunny rabbit'"[283], which points to Hagrid's fondness of dangerous creatures and the varying perspectives on Norbert.[284]

---

278 Cf. Roz Kaveney. "Dragons.", 295.; cf. "Dragons." in: David Leeming. *The Oxford Companion to World Mythology*, 106.

279 "Dragons." in: David Leeming. *The Oxford Companion to World Mythology*, 106.

280 Sandra Unerman. "Dragons in Twentieth Century Fiction.", 94.

281 Cf. ibid., 97. She also mentions the dragons used in the Triwizard Tournament in *Harry Potter and the Goblet of Fire* (2000). Cf. ibid.

282 Ibid.

283 J.K. Rowling. *Harry Potter and the Philosopher's Stone*, 173.

284 A further example to highlight the dynamic image of dragons is Nonesuch in Donn Kushner's *A Book Dragon* (1987). As the title already suggests, Nonesuch eventually

Notwithstanding their marginal role in Tolkien's *The Lord of the Rings*, several of his other works feature dragons "as real and very dangerous creatures, coldly calculating and fiercely intelligent"[285]. The diversity of dragons in Tolkien's works led scholars to differentiate between the dragon breeds that can be found in Middle-earth. Tyler distinguishes between "the fire-breathing sort, of high royalty" and "'cold-drakes' whose power [...] [lies] in strength and size alone"[286]. In spite of this distinction, he concludes that "all Dragons were large and heavily armoured, with long, coiling tails, and many could fly. And all were immensely strong, quick-witted, intellectual, greedy and callous beyond belief"[287]. Given that Tolkien's dragons are extremely vigorous and some of them even eloquent, they appear as dangerous, intelligent and deadly foes, as can be seen from the fact that three of his most renowned dragons follow this pattern.[288]

In his tale "Farmer Giles of Ham" (1949), Tolkien introduces the dragon Chrysophylax, who "was of ancient and imperial lineage, and very rich. He was cunning, inquisitive, greedy, well-armoured, but not over bold"[289] and, as Sandra Unerman notes, "a fire-breathing, treasure-loving beast but a coward"[290]. Chrysophylax is endowed with bestial characteristics, on which Tolkien already elaborated in his lecture on "Beowulf: The Monsters and the Critics". In this lecture, which was delivered in 1936, the Oxford professor claimed that the dragon in *Beowulf* appears to be a "plain pure fairy-story dragon"[291] and is reminiscent of 'draconitas' (dragon-like) rather than 'draco' (dragon), which is the "personification of malice, greed [and] destruction"[292]. With this statement, Tolkien places his own dragons in the realm of evil, where Chrysophylax and, even more so, Glaurung, one of the dragons in *The Silmarillion*, belong. When he was just a half-grown dragon, Glaurung made the elves flee from him and caused chaos and destruction in the fields of Ard-galen.[293] This image of malice

---

does not guard a hoard of gold but a book, which becomes his sole treasure; moreover, he refrains from eating humans, except when there is no alternative.

285 Mark Atherton. *There and Back Again*, 47.

286 "Dragons." in: J.E.A. Tyler. *The Tolkien Companion*, 108. In *The History of The Hobbit*, John D. Rateliff uses different parameters to distinguish the dragons and divides them into three groups: 1.) dragons "who remain undifferentiated from one another in the background of the stories, although their deeds *en masse* may be of importance", 2.) "dragons who are merely a name [...] or deed [...] but who are given no line of dialogue or any characteristic that would mark them as individual personalities", 3.) those "who are presented with fully developed personalities, true characters in their respective works". John D. Rateliff. *The History of The Hobbit*, 527-29, original emphasis.

287 "Dragons." in: J.E.A. Tyler. *The Tolkien Companion*, 108.

288 For a more detailed account on Tolkien's dragons see John D. Rateliff. *The History of The Hobbit*, 525-34.

289 J.R.R. Tolkien. "Farmer Giles of Ham.", 116.

290 Sandra Unerman. "Dragons in Twentieth Century Fiction.", 96.

291 J.R.R. Tolkien. "Beowulf: The Monsters and the Critics", n.p.

292 Ibid., n.p.

293 Cf. J.R.R. Tolkien. *The Silmarillion*, 132.

is intensified when he becomes the leader of Morgoth's army: "In the front of that fire came Glaurung the golden, father of dragons, in his full might; and in his train were Balrogs, and behind them came the black armies of the Orcs in multitudes such as the Noldor had never before seen or imagined"[294]. Hence, Glaurung is directly connected with the most powerful evil that can be found in Middle-earth, Morgoth and his dark forces of Orcs and Balrogs. The connection between dragon and evil is also hinted at in Peter Jackson's *The Desolation of Smaug*, in which Smaug is likewise associated with the most evil entity of Middle-earth in the Third Age, Sauron. When Bilbo encounters the dragon, Smaug's eye features Sauron's silhouette at one point, he mentions the increasing powers of Sauron, which indicates a relationship between the dragon and Sauron, and he refers to the One Ring. Smaug's awareness of the One Ring becomes apparent when he says, "'[t]here is something about you. Something you carry. Something made of gold. But far more precious. [Voice of the Ring] Precious! Precious!'"[295]. But even in Tolkien's original tale, Smaug's "basic function in the story is that of the traditional dragon, the evil enemy whose destruction brings about the happy ending"[296]. This can, for instance, be seen in his role as 'conqueror of Erebor' that attributes characteristics such as power and destruction to him and makes him appear as frightening and dangerous as possible.

3.2 The Dwarves' Antagonist: Smaug

After getting familiar with the dwarves and their history in the 'Song of the Lonely Mountain', many readers or listeners would expect an equally detailed introduction to the dragon and his usurpation of the dwarf kingdom – they are, however, disappointed. Although the second part of the song does not contain an extensive description of Smaug, the song, nevertheless, comprises other remarkable hints that allow conclusions about the dragon's character, "who is given one of the strongest portraits of any dragon in modern fiction"[297]. For instance, his characteristics can be seen in the way in which nature is destroyed and the images which were used to create a pleasant atmosphere in the first part are

294 J.R.R. Tolkien. *The Silmarillion*, 175.

295 Peter Jackson. *The Desolation of Smaug*, 01:50:44-01:51:04. He further states that "'Oakenshield's quest will fail. The darkness is coming. It will spread to every corner of the land'", which hints at Sauron's increasing powers. These are further highlighted in a cut from Erebor to Dol Guldur. Ibid., 01:58:15-01:58:54.

296 Sandra Unerman. "Dragons in Twentieth Century Fiction.", 96. Unerman's assumption that Smaug's death brings about the happy ending needs to be qualified, though, because Smaug's death first and foremost establishes the basis for the events leading up to the battle of the five armies. It is not only that "[t]he quarrels over his [Smaug's] hoard lead to as much trouble and danger for the hobbit as Smaug did when he was alive", but even to an actual war between different peoples. Ibid.

297 Ibid. Rudolf Simek also considers Smaug to be the dragon described in most detail in Tolkien's fiction. Cf. Rudolf Simek. *Mittelerde*, 134-35.

distorted. This is the reason why the transition from the first to the second part of the song is particularly relevant to its further analysis, since the parts are not separated by an intermediate chorus. Instead, the arrival of the dragon follows the most private stanza of the song. Corey Olsen notes that "[i]t is in the context of this privacy, this ownership of their treasure [introduced in the sixth stanza], that they speak of the invasion of the dragon and of his violation and destruction of their kingdom"[298]. Indeed, the song shifts from the depths of the dwarf kingdom to the destruction of the environment surrounding the mountain. The dragon is thus introduced at a point in time at which the dwarves' nostalgia is most intense, namely when they speak about their own (social) life within the mountain that was ended by the horror of the dragon's attack. Moreover, a special focus is put on the injustice they experienced; they were working in their halls and workshops when suddenly, for no apparent reason, the dragon appeared and destroyed what they had built. Consequently, "the focus [of the song] is entirely on the dwarvish victims rather than on the dragon who is killing them"[299], which reinforces that the song is bound to the dwarves' perspective.

Nevertheless, Smaug and his characteristics are first described indirectly in the destruction of nature surrounding the mountain. The dragon's raid is hinted at in the description of the trees: "'*The pines were roaring on the height*'"[300]. The trees that grow close to the mountain are evergreen conifers, which do not change their appearance with the seasons but require other elemental forces, such as wind or fire, to change them. The word "roaring" is characteristic of the dragon, not of pines or trees, and supports the claim that the dragon is indirectly referred to by the destruction of nature. Even though the second part is used to introduce Smaug, the dragon "is not a character in this poem"[301]. Nevertheless, this stanza contains another important aspect that is relevant to the introduction of Smaug, namely the dragon's nocturnal activity, which is indicated by the reference to his fiery attack during night-time.[302] Night-time in general evokes a rather eerie atmosphere and allows the dragon to attack under the cover of darkness, when his flames can be seen most distinctly. The scale of his devastation is more than just a local fire; the dragon sets everything ablaze and transforms the trees into torches, which illuminate the scene, and destroys the area around the mountain.[303]

---

298 Corey Olsen. *Exploring* The Hobbit, 32.

299 Ibid., 33.

300 Appendix: "Song of the Lonely Mountain", l. 25.

301 Corey Olsen. *Exploring* The Hobbit, 33.

302 Cf. Appendix: "Song of the Lonely Mountain", ll.26, 36. Christine Rauer notes that the dragon's "nocturnal nature" is a prominent feature in the Old English epic poem *Beowulf*. She explains that "[t]he *Beowulf*-poet seems to imply not only that the dragon is habitually active during the night and at dusk and dawn, but also (and more remarkably) that it is normally *asleep during the day*". Christine Rauer. *Beowulf and the Dragon*, 34, original emphasis.

303 Cf. Appendix: "Song of the Lonely Mountain", ll. 27-28.

The two remaining stanzas not only introduce other traits of the dragon, such as his wrath, but also reinforce his destructive nature, by using distorted images and comparisons with natural phenomena. For instance, the sound of ringing bells, which was caused by the hammering of the dwarves and also perceived as a familiar and pleasant sound, is transformed into a warning, by using almost the same terms: "'*[t]he bells were ringing in the dale*'"[304]. When the focus of the song shifts back towards Erebor, the dwarves sing that "'*[t]he mountain smoked beneath the moon*'"[305], which is an image reminiscent of a volcano, to which the dragon's fury is compared at a later point in the novel and which also implies havoc and devastation.[306] In addition, these stanzas pick up several images that are frequently associated with dragons, such as his ability to fly or to breathe fire, and that become a symbol of his wrath.[307]

In comparison with Thorin's prose account of the events, the song seems to omit or alter information. For instance, "the song never actually depicts Smaug the dragon"[308] or calls him by his name, nor does it explain the dragon's motives for attacking Erebor. Olsen even speculates that the dwarves "seem almost to want to avoid paying Smaug the compliment of making him the chief character of their story"[309], which is why they do not properly introduce Smaug in their song. Another aspect that makes the second part of the song different from Thorin's account is that the dragon's attack apparently affected only the exterior of the mountain, whereas its interior seems to be untouched by the dragon. In fact, the song never describes what happens when Smaug enters the mountain. This may be due to the fact that the dwarves reconstruct the place with the help of their collective memory, which is closely tied to their point of view, and more importantly, that the dwarves aim at mentally recreating a particular place, which they saw many years ago. Sometimes these places are idealised and glorified, as was shown in the reconstruction of the old kingdom. Thorin, on the other hand, recollects the events in his subsequent explanation from his personal point of view and the parts he witnessed. The intimacy of his descriptions can, for example, be seen in the pronoun 'we' that takes the place of the pronoun 'they' of the song. Therefore, it can be assumed that the dwarves revisit the destruction of the place whenever they sing the song, and that they have intentionally omitted a detailed description of their adversary or have been unable to provide one.

The first chapter offers more information on the dragon than the 'Song of the Lonely Mountain'. When Thorin explains that "'[d]ragons steal gold and jewels [...] from men and elves and dwarves, wherever they can find them; and they

---

304 Appendix: "Song of the Lonely Mountain", l. 29.

305 Ibid., l. 33.

306 Cf. J.R.R. Tolkien. *The Hobbit*, 251.

307 Cf. Appendix: "Song of the Lonely Mountain", ll. 25-27.

308 Corey Olsen. *Exploring* The Hobbit, 33.

309 Ibid.

guard their plunder as long as they live (which is practically for ever, unless they are killed)'"[310], he describes several important characteristics of them. The first is that dragons are attracted by gold, which makes them steal it from others and ascribes the role of thieves to them. The second is the dragon's longevity, which destroys the dwarves' hope that the dragon might be dead and emphasises that he is still "the frightful guardian"[311] of their treasure. Finally, he also gives the reason for the dragon's raid, namely greed. This topic has already been discussed in connection with the dwarves' desire for the treasure, and both sides share this characteristic. Tom Shippey even assumes an impact of the dragon on the treasure:

> At the bottom of it [dragon-sickness] there lies an old superstition which says that dragons are actually misers who have in greed and despair walled themselves up alive, 'lain down on their gold' as sagas say. Naturally the gold on which they have brooded [...] exudes a miasma of avarice.[312]

In this statement, he assumes that, in a way, the treasure is affected by the dragon and his greedy brooding and suggests that the gold (even after the dragon has left) can cause dragon-sickness.[313] However, this does not seem fully applicable in this case, because the dwarves are generally described as being in love with gold.[314] An example to illustrate this is when the company enters the trolls' lair and removes several pots of gold and buries them elsewhere; to ensure that they can recover these pots later they cast several spells on the treasure.[315] Consequently, the dwarves and the dragon share a similar love of gold, which may be reinforced by the considerable amount of treasure that is stored in the mountain. Shippey, however, has a point when he claims that "[t]here is in the final chapters a continuum of greed"[316]. The closer the dwarves get to the mountain and to their treasure, the more obvious their desire becomes; the more they stir up the dragon, the clearer his will to defend the gold becomes. For example, Smaug's avarice finds expression in his furious, destructive campaign after he has realised that a cup is missing from his hoard.[317]

---

310 J.R.R. Tolkien. *The Hobbit*, 28.

311 Ibid., 250.

312 Tom Shippey. *The Road to Middle-earth*, 101.

313 This is, for instance, also addressed in C.S. Lewis' *The Voyage of the Dawn Treader* (1952), in which Eustace Scrubb comes across a treasure in a dragon's cave and is turned into a dragon when he sleeps on the hoard. As soon as Eustace realises that he has become a dragon, the narrator explains that "[s]leeping on a dragon's hoard with greedy, dragonish thoughts in his heart" is the reason why "he had become a dragon himself". C.S. Lewis. *The Voyage of the Dawn Treader*, 97.

314 Cf. J.R.R. Tolkien. *The Hobbit*, 276-77.

315 Cf. ibid., 52.

316 Tom Shippey. *The Road to Middle-earth*, 100.

317 Cf. J.R.R. Tolkien. *The Hobbit*, 252-55.

In Peter Jackson's final part of the trilogy the idea of greed or rather 'dragon-sickness' is drawn upon in several scenes. At the beginning of *The Battle of the Five Armies*, the Master of Lake-town greedily loads his boat with items from his treasure chamber when the dragon attacks. Before he is able to escape from Lake-town, he is killed by Smaug, who has been shot by a black arrow and falls dead from the sky.[318] Killed in poetic justice, the Master is punished for his greed, because he values gold and precious items more than the lives of the citizens of Lake-town. Apart from the Master of Lake-town, Thorin Oakenshield, who is gradually infected by dragon-sickness, is another example of a character affected by treasure. When the company searches for the Arkenstone, Thorin mistakes the acorn Bilbo has collected in Beorn's garden for the gemstone, tells Bilbo that he has been betrayed by his own kin and suspects that one of them has taken the Arkenstone.[319] These depictions of avarice are intensified when Thorin's voice begins to resemble the voice of the dragon; when his voice shifts, it becomes apparent that he is no longer his own master, but is affected by dragon-sickness. Thorin's avarice is most intense when he goes into "'the Gallery of the Kings'"[320], in which the floor is – due to the collapsing of the dwarf statue at the end of *The Desolation of Smaug* – covered with gold. While several voices in the background indicate that Thorin is turning mad, he sees the dragon sliding like a sea-serpent beneath the shining golden floor and imagines himself to be drawn into a swirl of gold and ultimately swallowed by the surface. After this incident he is able to recognise that he was in thrall to the gold and tosses his crown, which is part of his family inheritance, on the ground.[321] Hence, Peter Jackson deliberately chose the dragon in combination with gold to highlight the characters' greed.

In Tolkien's *The Hobbit*, greed for gold forms an important part of Smaug's personality that is even reflected in his description as "'a most specially greedy, strong and wicked worm'"[322]. The superlative indicates that his greed is abnormal, even in comparison to other (literary) dragons, which are considered to be "emblems of covetousness"[323]. Furthermore, it highlights that Smaug's strength and his malice contribute to making him the evil and dangerous adversary the company has to defeat eventually. Sandra Unerman observes that "[w]e are told a great deal about him before we ever meet him, of the fear and destruction he has caused and his greed for treasure"[324], which are already hinted at in the 'Song of the Lonely Mountain'.

318 Cf. Peter Jackson. *The Battle of the Five Armies*, 00:10:35-00:10:48.

319 Cf. ibid., 00:35:10-00:36:17, 00:48:02-00:48:46.

320 Peter Jackson. *The Desolation of Smaug*, 02:21:30-02:21:31.

321 Cf. Peter Jackson. *The Battle of the Five Armies*, 01:19:26-01:21:17.

322 J.R.R. Tolkien. *The Hobbit*, 29.

323 Roz Kaveney. "Dragons.", 295.

324 Sandra Unerman. "Dragons in Twentieth Century Fiction.", 96.

In *Tolkien's Art*, Jane Chance analyses Smaug's wickedness in the context of the seven deadly sins. She notes that Smaug "expresses 'spiritual sin' chiefly through his pride, although he also manifests wrath, avarice, and envy"[325]. Most of these characteristics are already indicated by his name, 'Smaug the Golden', which hints in particular at his greedy nature. In a letter to the editor of the 'Observer', Tolkien explains that "[t]he dragon bears as name – a pseudonym – the past tense of the primitive Germanic verb *Smugan*, to squeeze through a hole: a low philological jest"[326]. Therefore, it is no coincidence that Smaug conquers the dwarf kingdom, which is situated in a mountain and resembles a hole in the earth. His epithet 'the Golden' connects him with the treasure that the dwarves have hoarded in the depths of the mountain and is also a symbol of his nobility and pride.[327] His self-appointed title 'King under the Mountain' becomes the symbol of both his pride and envy. This title does originally belong to Thorin, who is heir to the throne of Erebor, but as soon as Smaug conquered the mountain, he has also taken the title and becomes 'king'.[328] In the chapter "Fire and Water", the narrative suggests that the inhabitants of Esgaroth apparently make a distinction between Smaug and Thorin when referring to the 'King under the Mountain': when the watchmen hope that "'the King under the Mountain is forging gold'"[329] a capitalised 'K' is used to refer to Thorin, whereas when Bard considers Smaug as "'the only king under the Mountain we have ever known'"[330] the semantic nuance is alluded to by means of the lower-case letter.[331] This indicates that the people in Lake-town use 'king' as a means to refer

325 Jane Chance. *Tolkien's Art*, 57-58.

326 Humphrey Carpenter (Ed.). *Letters of J.R.R. Tolkien*, 31 [Letter 25: To the editor of the 'Observer', February 1938], original emphasis. Rudolf Simek traces the origins of the word back to the perfect tense of the Old Norse *smjúga* ("sich schmiegen, sich zwängen", to squeeze in), which is *smaug* ("ist eingedrungen", penetrated, invaded). Rudolf Simek. *Mittelerde*, 134.

327 This epithet can also be associated with his appearance as "a vast red-golden dragon". J.R.R. Tolkien. *The Hobbit*, 249. Arguably, the mixture of both would make him appear rather copper-coloured, as can also be seen in Tolkien's illustration "Conversation with Smaug". Cf. Douglas A. Anderson. *Das große Hobbit Buch*, n.p.

328 Jane Chance also notes that "Tolkien calls his dragon Smaug 'King under the Mountain' because under a mountain he guards a treasure that he wrongfully stole from previous Dwarf-kings". Jane Chance. *Tolkien's Art*, 54.

329 J.R.R. Tolkien. *The Hobbit*, 285.

330 Ibid., 286.

331 Only at one point is Bard's reference to "'the true king under the Mountain'" marked with a lower-case letter. In this case, however, it is not used to refer to Thorin specifically. Ibid., 289. This instance shows Bard's attitude towards the dwarf king, in whom he does not fully believe, because he only knows the dragon as king inside the mountain. Cf. ibid., 286. This temporal gap is also addressed by Corey Olsen, who maintains that "[g]enerations of the Lake dwellers have lived and died since Smaug laid waste to the Mountain and to Dale, and the events are now regarded as ancient legends". Corey Olsen. *Exploring* The Hobbit, 185.

to Erebor's fiery inhabitant; they do not use it as a proper title, thus refraining from acknowledging the dragon as the king of the former dwarf kingdom. Even though Smaug considers himself 'King' and wants Bilbo to believe this, the people near the mountainside have a different opinion, which is expressed in this detail.

In addition to his title, several other "spiritual sin[s]"[332] can be found in more general descriptions of Smaug. Tyler, for instance, describes his cunning behaviour, his fearsome wrath and his vanity, to pin down the evil nature of the dragon.[333] Olsen goes even further in describing Smaug as a monstrous and cruel dragon, who is responsible for the massacre that drove the dwarves out of Erebor.[334] These draconic traits are also referred to in descriptions of the dragon in the story. For instance, Smaug's greed manifests itself in his waistcoat of diamonds and jewels, through which he has literally become a part of the treasure and which is the reason for his vanity ("'Yes, it is rare and wonderful, indeed,' said Smaug *absurdly pleased*"[335]) that ultimately leads to his death.[336]

His vanity finds expression in another and arguably his most dangerous ability, namely the ability to speak.[337] Therefore, Ármann Jakobsson is right to claim that Smaug's behaviour and speech are exceptional for a dragon and that the way he speaks makes him "clever and subtle and formidable in an eerie way"[338]. He argues that "[t]he moment it speaks, it becomes a character, an intelligent person who is not merely governed by his bestial instincts. The dragon still retains these bestial instincts, though"[339]. Smaug's ambivalent nature is the basis on which Tom Shippey concludes that

> [t]he paradoxes, the oscillations between animal and intelligent behaviour, the contrast between creaky politeness of speech and plain gloating over murder, all help to give Smaug

332 Jane Chance. *Tolkien's Art*, 58.

333 Cf. "Smaug the Golden." in: J.E.A. Tyler. *The Tolkien Companion*, 445.

334 Cf. Corey Olsen. *Exploring* The Hobbit, 37.

335 J.R.R. Tolkien. *The Hobbit*, 262, my emphasis.

336 The parallel between Smaug's waistcoat and Bilbo's mithril coat is striking: even Bilbo experiences a moment of vanity when he is wearing the coat and considers how magnificent he looks. In contrast to Smaug, Bilbo discards these thoughts almost immediately when he thinks about how ridiculous he must appear in the eyes of his fellow hobbits. Cf. ibid., 278. However, Smaug's vanity can also be seen in his use of the treasure, because he is constantly surrounded by gold and precious objects, so that terms like "costly bed" or "golden couch" feature prominently when he is lying on the gold. Ibid., 250, 254.

337 In this respect, Smaug clearly resembles Fafnir, who is also able to speak. As Emily Midkiff observes, "[t]he dragons also use language to fight for the speaking, dominant role, as can be seen in the *verbal battle* that occurs at the death of the dragon Fáfnir". Emily Midkiff. "Uncanny Dragons.", 46, my emphasis. Tolkien admitted that Bilbo's conversation with the dragon is modelled on Fafnir. Cf. Humphrey Carpenter (Ed.). *Letters of J.R.R. Tolkien*, 134 [Letter 122: To Naomi Mitchison, December 1949].

338 Ármann Jakobsson. "Talk to the Dragon.", 29.

339 Ibid., 28.

his dominant characteristic of 'wiliness', and what the narrator calls with utter modernity […] his 'overwhelming personality'.[340]

This "wiliness" enables Smaug to talk on a highly intellectual level and to raise doubts about the credibility of the dwarves as well as their quest and allows him to manipulate Bilbo. Smaug has acquired the human ability to speak, so he is half-animal and half-human: "[t]he dragon is no longer merely terrible and bestial, he now also becomes uncanny, strange and yet familiar, human and yet not human"[341]. In his article "Monster Theory (Seven Theses)", Jeffrey Jerome Cohen elaborates on the impossibility of assigning monsters to (clear-cut) categories in his third thesis and argues:

> This refusal to participate in the classificatory 'order of things' is true of monsters generally: they are disturbing hybrids whose externally incoherent bodies resist attempts to include them in any systematic structuration. And so the monster is dangerous, a form suspended between forms that threatens to smash distinctions.[342]

Smaug's hybrid nature and the danger he poses to the hobbit can be seen in his self-description when he brags to the burglar: "'My armour is like tenfold shields, my teeth are swords, my claws spears, the shock of my tail a thunderbolt, my wings a hurricane, and my breath death!'"[343]. Smaug not only inspires the reader to imagine a most cruel creature but also, more importantly, compares himself to natural forces as well as human weaponry to highlight his hybridity. The comparison with weapons and armour, such as shields, swords and spears, hints at both his seemingly incredible strength as well as the dwarves' present lack of weaponry, which makes them even more vulnerable to an attack by the dragon. By contrast, the forces of nature, such as a thunderbolt or a hurricane, refer back to the second part of the 'Song of the Lonely Mountain', in which the dragon was introduced by wind and flames. This also applies to his fiery breath, with which he, for instance, killed the dwarves that tried to escape from the

340 Tom Shippey. *The Road to Middle-earth*, 103.

341 Ármann Jakobsson. "Talk to the Dragon.", 34. In addition, Tom Shippey notes that "nothing could be more archaic or fantastic than a dragon brooding on its gold, and yet the strong sense of familiarity in this one's speech puts it back into the 'continuum of greed', makes it just dimly possible that dragon-motivations could on their different scale have some affinity with human ones – even real historical human ones". Tom Shippey. *The Road to Middle-earth*, 104. This similarity between monsters and human beings was also noticed by Emily Midkiff, who explains that this similarity makes them so terrifying: she argues that it is "the dragons' intensely possessive gaze and their clever, manipulative speech" that makes them appear dangerous and uncanny. Emily Midkiff. "Uncanny Dragons.", 43.

342 Jeffrey Jerome Cohen. "Monster Culture (Seven Theses).", 6.

343 J.R.R. Tolkien. *The Hobbit*, 262.

mountain during his attack and were incinerated by his deadly breath.[344] Thus, in comparison to the other monsters that Bilbo and the company encounter, the dragon is by far the most vicious creature they have to face. His persuasive speech as well as his human behaviour add to his potentially uncanny and fearsome appearance.[345] Consequently, it is the mixture of spoken words, greed, fire, destruction, fury and retribution that is the dragon's most dangerous and most deadly weapon, but also, as it turns out, the most self-destructive and ultimately fatal one.

3.3 Eerie, Creepy and Dangerous: The Dragon's Lair

Despite the fact that Smaug's uncanny appearance has already been addressed in scholarly works, the dragon's lair is almost always left out. This is the reason why I would like to argue that the eerie atmosphere is created not only by the dragon's gaze or his intelligent and manipulative demeanour but also by the description of his 'lair' within the mountain. The description of Erebor when Smaug inhabits the halls of the former kingdom is characterised by a tension between the halls' 'glorious' past state and their present appearance. The descriptions of the mountain's interior contain elements typically found in Gothic fiction and hint at a transformation by blending the past and present appearance in some artefacts and objects.

The tension between its former and present state is reminiscent of what Jane Suzanne Carroll describes as the 'chthonic space':

> Caves, graves, and holes in the ground open up and expose the buried layers of both time and space, making the chronotopic correlation between time and space apparent without the need for excavation. [...] The chthonic space, therefore, becomes synonymous with the relationship between past and present.[346]

She also refers to *The Hobbit* and argues that the Lonely Mountain is a cave that is connected with the past:

> archaeology (the mention of artefacts) and genealogy (the mention of long-dead nobles) both occur as signifiers of the past, but Tolkien maintains the integrity of the chthonic space as the true vehicle of the past by setting both the hoard and the conversations about it, within a cave.[347]

In *The Hobbit*, this temporal tension, however, is not restricted to the interior of the mountain (where it plays a prominent role), but also hinted at in the descrip-

---

[344] Cf. Appendix: "Song of the Lonely Mountain", ll. 35-36. Bilbo even comes to feel the dragon's fiery breath when it singes the hair on his feet. Cf. J.R.R. Tolkien. *The Hobbit*, 264.

[345] Cf. Ármann Jakobsson. "Talk to the Dragon.", 34.

[346] Jane Suzanne Carroll. *Landscape in Children's Literature*, 141.

[347] Ibid., 148.

tions of the mountain's surroundings and in particular the depiction of the natural environment and landscape: "The land about them grew bleak and barren, though once, as Thorin told them, it had been green and fair. There was little grass, and before long there was neither bush nor tree, and only broken and blackened stumps to speak of ones long vanished"[348]. The depiction of a wasteland as opposed to the formerly fair lands hints at the fact that the land has not yet fully recovered from Smaug's attack. The "broken and blackened stumps" indicate that nature either did not regrow, or, what seems even more likely, became subject to several further dragon attacks. The "bleak and barren" country is reminiscent of the dragon's former habitat, the Withered Heath, which is "[a] desolate region in the eastern range of the Grey Mountains"[349]. The desolation of the mountain's surroundings is emphasised in Tolkien's illustration 'The Front Gate'[350], which conveys a dismal atmosphere. The illustration suggests that the area surrounding the mountain is completely barren and dangerous; stones protrude from the gloomy river and, apart from one tree stump, only a single withered tree can be seen. The description of the mountain's surroundings also highlights an observation made by Liam Campbell: "Whether rich in floral beauty or ragged and wild, all across the wide panorama of his tales and verse Tolkien consistently foregrounded place and nature"[351]. The comparison between the former state of the environment surrounding the mountain and the descriptions (and illustration) of its present state indicate that not only place and nature are in the focus but also that the temporal dimension plays an important role. In this respect, the place is "like a palimpsest, with ruins that are traces bearing witness to earlier, erased, suppressed or forgotten 'texts,' i.e. histories and life situations"[352].

The area surrounding the Lonely Mountain is further characterised by a lack of movement: "[n]othing moved in the waste, save the vapour and the water, and every now and again a black and ominous crow"[353]. In spite of these few exceptions, the movement of the vapour, the water and the crow do not contribute to a pleasant feeling in the waste. The vapour is reminiscent of the fog in the Misty Mountains and the crow is connected with darkness as well as danger and frequently seen as a symbol of death. The surroundings are passive and have been transformed into a "perilous waste"[354], which barely changed over the course of time. With focus on the wasteland as a setting, John D. Rateliff explains: "One of the more interesting bits of Tolkien's dragon-lore, as presented in *The Hobbit* and elsewhere, is the idea that dragons are not only found in desolate places [...],

348 J.R.R. Tolkien. *The Hobbit*, 235.
349 "Withered Heath." in: J.E.A. Tyler. *The Tolkien Companion*, 524.
350 J.R.R. Tolkien. *The Hobbit*, 237.
351 Liam Campbell. "Nature.", 435.
352 Nicole Schröder. *Spaces and Places in Motion*, 44.
353 J.R.R. Tolkien. *The Hobbit*, 236.
354 Ibid., 238.

but that they make places desolate simply by dwelling in them"[355]. Thus, either the dragon's attack laid waste to the area and is responsible for its appearance as a desolate and barren country, or the presence of the dragon transformed the area into a social wasteland, which is devoid of men, elves and dwarves as well as animals (except for the dragon or occasionally some crows) – or it may even be a mixture of both.

Despite its bleak appearance, the area is also connected with hope. Hope is, for instance, expressed in the "little steep-walled bay, grassy-floored, still and quiet"[356], which becomes the dwarves' hide-out from Smaug. This "grassy bay"[357] contrasts the desolation and waste caused by the dragon. Before long, however, this symbol of hope is destroyed by the rampaging beast, when "[h]is hot breath shrivelled the grass before the door"[358]. A further, probably more potent symbol of hope is the old thrush. Olsen notes that "[t]he thrush is a symbol of the harmony of the old days, when dwarves and men were at peace and even the wise and goodly birds were 'tame to the hands' of Thorin's father and grandfather"[359]. Even though the thrush plays a crucial role in revealing the key hole, its appearance is rather dismal: "[t]here on the grey stone in the grass was an enormous thrush, nearly coal black, its pale yellow breast freckled with dark spots"[360]. At one point, Bilbo puts forward in a bad temper: "'I believe he is listening, and I don't like the look of him'"[361], which contributes to a slightly ambiguous perception of the bird. For the dwarves, however, the thrush is linked with the old days and the former kingdom and remains a symbol of hope.

The gloomy atmosphere in the desolation is evoked by Gothic elements that have been implemented in the descriptions of the mountain's exterior. Despite the fact that Mary Ellen Snodgrass lists *The Hobbit* among the "Major Works of Gothic fiction"[362], I refrain from analysing the novel in the context of Gothic literature and just focus on some elements that were prominently used in Gothic texts. Andrew Smith lists some of them:

> Despite the national, formal, and generic mutations of the Gothic, it is possible to identify certain persistent features which constitute a distinctive aesthetic. Representations of ruins, castles, monasteries, and forms of monstrosity, and images of insanity, transgression, the supernatural, and excess, all typically characterise the form.[363]

---

355 John D. Rateliff. *The History of The Hobbit*, 483.

356 J.R.R. Tolkien. *The Hobbit*, 239.

357 Ibid., 243.

358 Ibid., 254. The significance of the grass is further emphasised when Bilbo remarks that "'[t]he dragon has withered all the pleasant green'". Ibid., 266.

359 Corey Olsen. *Exploring* The Hobbit, 224.

360 J.R.R. Tolkien. *The Hobbit*, 243.

361 Ibid., 264.

362 Cf. Mary E. Snodgrass. *Encyclopedia of Gothic Literature*, 381.

363 Andrew Smith. *Gothic Literature*, 4.

The most obvious connection to the elements Smith lists as characteristic of Gothic literature is the setting. Both Dale and Erebor have been turned into ruins, as can be seen when Balin sadly remarks that "'[t]here lies all that is left of Dale'"[364], which indicates that only remnants of the formerly prosperous city exist. The same applies to the ancient halls of the dwarf kingdom that have been destroyed by the marauding dragon and which contain objects that hint at the destruction.[365] In this respect, Erebor bears a striking resemblance to Khazad-dûm, which contained "'*many-pillared halls of stone / With golden roof and silver floor*'"[366], as Gimli points out in his song, but which became a tomb for many dwarves and has been taken over by orcs.[367] The parallels between both places are obvious and highlight the strong contrast between the Balrog/Smaug and the dwarves. In addition to the setting, "monstrosity" can be found in the creatures the company encounters. These comprise, for instance, the destructive and manipulating nature of "Tolkien's menacing breed"[368], Smaug, but also the creature Gollum or the goblins in Goblin-town.[369]

These Gothic elements are further elaborated on when the dragon's lair is described. The personification of the mountain as a crucial part of the body metaphor has already been introduced and is drawn upon again when Thorin and his company manage to open the secret door to the hidden passage in the mountain, which creates a gloomy first impression of the dragon's lair. This entrance is described as "a yawning mouth leading in and down"[370], which is an image that is reminiscent of the hell-mouth and which anticipates that the dragon is waiting at the end of the darkness. Furthermore, it evokes the idea that both the hobbit and later also the dwarf company are swallowed by the mountain, especially after the door needs to be shut and the feeling of claustrophobia increases.[371]

---

364 J.R.R. Tolkien. *The Hobbit*, 236. In fact, Dale is actually referred to as a 'ruin'/'ruins' four times in the novel. Cf. ibid., 26, 62, 236, 289.

365 For example, this becomes apparent in the tall arch the company comes across after the dragon left its lair and which is "worn and splintered and blackened". Ibid., 280. Descriptions like this indicate that the interior of Erebor is as ruinous and dilapidated as Dale.

366 J.R.R. Tolkien. *The Fellowship of the Ring*, 412, original emphasis.

367 Cf. ibid., 412-13. Since Gimli remembers Moria in a song, it can be assumed that he, just like the dwarves in *The Hobbit*, glorifies the appearance of the halls.

368 Emily Midkiff. "Uncanny Dragons.", 42.

369 At least to some extent, Peter Jackson's adaptation also depicts a form of insanity by elaborating on the idea of 'dragon-sickness' that afflicted in particular Thorin's grandfather Thror. Cf. Peter Jackson. *The Desolation of Smaug*, 01:57:30-01:57:36.

370 J.R.R. Tolkien. *The Hobbit*, 245.

371 The idea of swallowing something or being swallowed is picked up several times in both the novel and Peter Jackson's adaptations: 'swallowing' is implied in the wood-elf realm, where the company is forced to enter the wood-elf king's dwelling through what Bilbo perceives as a "cavern-mouth", and in connection with the corpse of Smaug, who is swallowed by the lake. Furthermore, *An Unexpected Journey* features a swallowing sound when Thror tries to save the Arkenstone, which accidentally falls out of his hands and

The atmosphere of gloom is partially resolved when the interior of the mountain is described in more detail:

> This was no goblin entrance, or rough wood-elves' cave. It was a passage made by dwarves, at the height of their wealth and skill: straight as a ruler, smooth-floored and smooth-sided, going with a gentle never-varying slope direct – to some distant end in the blackness below.[372]

The comparison to the entrances built by goblins and elves reinforces the dwarves' skill once more. The 'entrance' into the goblin caves is merely "[a] crack [that] had opened at the back of the cave"[373] and appears to be functional rather than elaborate. By contrast, the entrance into the woodland realm consists of "huge doors of stone"[374], whose appearance remains unspecified. The focus on the dwarves' skill, thus, briefly distracts from the dangers that lurk at the bottom of the tunnel and stresses the idea of a 'homecoming' of the dwarves, who are returning to the halls and chambers of their ancestors.

The fact that the descriptions of Erebor feature Gothic elements can further be seen in the use of the term "'*dungeons*'"[375], with which the reader is familiar from the 'Song of the Lonely Mountain' and which reappears as "dungeon-hall"[376] when Bilbo goes down the tunnel to explore the ancient halls. When the dragon occupies the "'*hollow halls*'"[377] at the bottom of the tunnel, they are different from the time when the dwarves inhabited them. During the dwarves' occupation of the mountain, these halls were the emblem of their majestic architecture and were often filled with song. The presence of the dragon in these halls, however, causes "dreadful echoes"[378], and his menacing presence instils fear in the company. The dwarves even refuse to go further down the tunnel, because "they feared some cunning devilry of his [Smaug's]"[379].

Whether a place is perceived as frightful depends on the perspective of the character. Ricardo Gullón argues that "[s]pace [...] is filled with memories and hopes which in some way allows it to be personified, felt as a reality whose consistence varies according to who observes it or experiences it"[380]. While Bilbo perceives the place as what it is, namely a dragon's lair, Thorin's perspective differs greatly. After the dragon has left the mountain to destroy Esgaroth,

---

vanishes in the sea of gold. Cf. J.R.R. Tolkien. *The Hobbit*, 199, 290.; cf. Peter Jackson. *An Unexpected Journey*, 00:06:40.

372 J.R.R. Tolkien. *The Hobbit*, 247-48.

373 Ibid., 71.

374 Ibid., 194.

375 Appendix: "Song of the Lonely Mountain", l. 2.

376 J.R.R. Tolkien. *The Hobbit*, 249.

377 Appendix: "Song of the Lonely Mountain", l. 8.

378 J.R.R. Tolkien. *The Hobbit*, 251.

379 Ibid., 271.

380 Ricardo Gullón. "On Space in the Novel.", 12.

Thorin refers to Erebor twice as "'palace'"[381], which it once was. Corey Olsen notices a change in perception in the dwarves and especially Thorin and claims that "[a]t the beginning of the chapter ['Not at Home'], Thorin himself is feeling suffocated in the oppressive closeness of the dark tunnel [...]. Once Thorin has the long-lost wealth of his people in his hands again, the situation is altogether different"[382]. He further notes that throughout the chapter, "Thorin [...] now feels that *he* has returned home, and throughout the rest of the chapter, Bilbo is continually attempting to remind Thorin that he is 'not at home,' but rather in the lair of the dragon"[383]. The different points of view are highlighted when Bilbo refers to the dragon's lair as a "'nasty clockless, timeless hole'"[384]. His feeling of unease is shared by Bombur, who refers to Erebor as "'a cold lonesome place'"[385], though not by Thorin. In this context, it is crucial to take into consideration that "Bifur, Bofur, and Bombur were descended from Dwarves of Moria but were not of Durin's line"[386] and may thus have different attitudes towards Erebor. The difference in Thorin's and Bilbo's perspectives derives (at least partly) from "memories and hopes"[387], because Thorin has lived in Erebor before and remembers the ancient kingdom, whereas Bilbo does not share these experiences. In comparison with the other dwarves, Thorin arguably associates stronger feelings with Erebor, because he is the rightful heir and King under the Mountain.

The artefacts the company discovers when they explore the place after the dragon has left imply that Erebor has been subject to destruction and transformation. "They passed through the ruined chamber. Tables were rotting there; chairs and benches were lying there overturned, charred and decaying. Skulls and bones were upon the floor among flagons and bowls and broken drinking-horns and dust"[388]. This is a striking example of how the dragon and also time affected the objects in the mountain. In the previous chapter, I examined the 'Song of the Lonely Mountain' and its transition from the depiction of the dwarf kingdom to the dragon's attack, which follows one of the most private stanzas, i.e., the description of precious objects as well as songs and feasting. Especially the latter aspect is highlighted in the quotation that describes the chamber, as the tables, chairs and benches as well as the flagons, bowls and drinking horns are

---

381 J.R.R. Tolkien. *The Hobbit*, 278, 282. When the fellowship explores Moria in *The Fellowship of the Ring*, Gimli's perspective also deviates from the one of his companions: he refers to Moria as "'the great realm and city of the Dwarrowdelf'", whereas Sam and the rest of the company can only see "'darksome holes'". J.R.R. Tolkien. *The Fellowship of the Ring*, 411.

382 Corey Olsen. *Exploring* The Hobbit, 230.

383 Ibid., 231, original emphasis.

384 J.R.R. Tolkien. *The Hobbit*, 281.

385 Ibid., 282.

386 J.R.R. Tolkien. *The Return of the King*, 1418, asterisk note.

387 Ricardo Gullón. "On Space in the Novel.", 12.

388 J.R.R. Tolkien. *The Hobbit*, 279-80.

objects associated with community and feasting. They are remnants that still indicate their former use and function and which have been subject to decay and destruction. In their present state these objects are connected with the past; the dust, the bones and skulls highlight the time that has passed. This temporal gap is also apparent in the bridge that was used to cross the stream in the old days and which is now in ruins: "The bridge that Balin had spoken of they found long fallen, and most of its stones were now only boulders in the shallow noisy stream"[389]. Descriptions like the ones mentioned above reinforce the idea that the place is different from what it looked before, while simultaneously giving some indication as to what the dwarves had originally built inside the mountain.

In the context of the gap between the past and present state of the mountain, the front gate plays a prominent role. During their exploration, the company comes across this gate: "They explored the caverns once more, and found, as they expected, that only the Front Gate remained open; all the other gates (except, of course, the small secret door) had long ago been broken and blocked by Smaug, and no sign of them remained"[390]. Unlike the other doors in the mountain, this door has not been smashed but is still used as a door by Smaug to leave Erebor. Smaug, who is compared to "a monstrous crow"[391], has been sitting in his 'nest' and left his 'aviary' through the gate that he used to conquer the dwarf kingdom in the first place. In his analysis of the front gate, Corey Olsen assigns another, symbolic meaning to it: "The gate is given special significance by the fact that the River Running flows out of it from its subterranean well-spring. Figuratively, the life and well-being of the whole region flowed from the open gate of the King under the Mountain"[392]. This turns out to be different when the dragon inhabits the mountain: it is no longer gold or wealth that comes out of the mountain but the dragon and his fiery breath.

Even though the dragon has entered the mountain, destroyed the dwarf kingdom and turned it into a dragon's lair, Erebor becomes subject to a further reshaping. After the raven Roäc informed Thorin and his company that Smaug is dead, the dwarves almost immediately "began to labour hard in fortifying the main entrance, and in making a new path that led from it"[393]. Attempting to prevent anyone from entering the mountain again, the dwarves alter the appearance of the place and even build something 'new'. Working with the tools which used to belong to their ancestors the dwarves "contrived a small low arch under the new wall" and "altered the narrow bed"[394] of the river and actively engage in reshaping the interior of the mountain. When the armies of men and elves approach the mountain, they see "the Gate blocked with a wall of *new*-hewn

---

389 J.R.R. Tolkien. *The Hobbit*, 282.

390 Ibid., 301.

391 Ibid., 269.

392 Corey Olsen. *Exploring* The Hobbit, 255.

393 J.R.R. Tolkien. *The Hobbit*, 301.

394 Ibid., 302.

stone"[395]. Olsen concludes that "Thorin's immovable gate is the perfect symbol of Thorin's kingdom so far, and it falls well short of anyone's hopes for the restoration of the kingdom of old"[396]. It seems as if the dichotomy between old and new as well as past and present is irreconcilable.

In this context, the song the dwarves sing once the armies of elves and men have come closer to the mountain is significant, as "Thorin's own mindset is clearly articulated in the song"[397]. This song is reminiscent of the 'Song of the Lonely Mountain' and repeats a few of its lines while simultaneously shifting the focus to new issues. One of the most striking stanzas to highlight the change in focus is the second stanza: "'*The sword is sharp, the spear is long, / The arrow swift, the Gate is strong; / The heart is bold that looks on gold; / The dwarves no more shall suffer wrong*'"[398]. The emphasis on warfare, avarice and the wrong the dwarves have experienced indicates that Thorin will defend his reclaimed halls. In this context, Corey Olsen makes a crucial observation, namely that "the stanza about harps and song has been squeezed into a single line in order to make room for a full stanza in praise of weaponry and declaring their resolution to 'suffer wrong' no more"[399]. The shift in focus from the former glory of the kingdom of old towards a war for the mountain implies that Thorin cannot simply rebuild Thrain's kingdom, which is indirectly referred to in the use of the present and the past tense in the song.

3.4 Peter Jackson's Visual Destruction and Reshaping of Erebor

The seizure and destruction of Erebor are explained in Thorin's retrospective account of the events that happened long ago. However, the description that Smaug "'crept in through the Front Gate and routed out all the halls, and lanes, and tunnels, alleys, cellars, mansions and passages'"[400] is not as detailed as readers (or film makers) might wish. Thus, similar to the visual creation of Erebor, Tolkien's descriptions leave room for Peter Jackson and his team to destroy the dwarf kingdom that they established previously. Its destruction is part of Bilbo's frame narrative, which is based on Thorin's explanation in *The Hobbit* and highlights Smaug's cruelty as well as his destructive powers.[401]

In line with the presentation of the order of settings in the 'Song of the Lonely Mountain', the exterior of the mountain is destroyed first. The pines are literally

---

395 J.R.R. Tolkien. *The Hobbit*, 303, my emphasis.
396 Corey Olsen. *Exploring* The Hobbit, 256.
397 Ibid., 252.
398 J.R.R. Tolkien, *The Hobbit*, 304.
399 Corey Olsen. *Exploring* The Hobbit, 254.
400 J.R.R. Tolkien, *The Hobbit*, 29.
401 Similar to the descriptions in the 'Song of the Lonely Mountain', Smaug is never shown completely: during Bilbo's frame narrative, the viewer does not even get a glimpse of his head and merely sees his extremities.

blown down by the wind caused by the dragon's wings, which changes the appearance of the mountainside, reinforcing the impression that a "'hurricane'"[402] might have swept across the wood. In this context, Smaug is even compared to natural forces[403], which highlights his animalistic nature and the fact that the dwarves do not stand a chance against him.[404] Unlike the dragon's attack in the dwarves' song, the attack takes place during the day, so that the effect of trees transformed into torches is not as impressive; the trees are, however, similar to what Bilbo hears in Thorin's explanation, "'creaking and cracking'"[405] on the mountainside. At the beginning of the dragon's attack, the golden banners on the railing of the fortress are in the focus and are soon perishing in the flames when the dragon comes down and attacks the mountain, which already anticipates the events yet to come.[406] When the camera shifts to Dale, the city is turned to ruins by the rampaging dragon and his fire within only a couple of minutes.[407] The speed with which the city is destroyed and turned into a ruin also suggests that most of the people were unable to escape the dragon.

When the camera pans back to the mountain, Erebor is still about to be destroyed. The front gate, which Olsen assigned a special significance to,[408] features prominently and is destroyed in the course of the attack. A close-up of the golden gate reveals its decorations;[409] its appearance suggests that this is the entrance to one of the most wealthy dwarf kingdoms in Middle-earth. Apart from being painted in gold, the gate is also richly ornamented with dwarf runes and decorated with red gemstones, which make the gate appear extremely valuable and elaborate in its design, so that it represents both the culture of the

402 Peter Jackson. *An Unexpected Journey*, 00:04:34. In *The Hobbit*, Smaug is also compared to a hurricane. Cf. J.R.R. Tolkien. *The Hobbit*, 29.

403 Concept Artist John Howe claims that "Smaug's attack on Erebor [...] has all the hallmarks of a natural disaster, something totally unstoppable: an avalanche, a forest fire, or a flood in the shape of this huge scaly Dragon". Qtd. in: Brian Sibley. *The Desolation of Smaug – Official Movie Guide*, 160.

404 The same applies to the inhabitants of Lake-town at the beginning of Jackson's *The Battle of the Five Armies*: enraged, Smaug leaves the mountain and heads towards Lake-town, which he begins to destroy immediately. Similar to the destruction of Dale, the ringing of a bell comes along with panic among the people. They are aware that the dragon causes destruction and that they have no chance of escaping his wrath. The Master of Lake-town even claims that "'[t]hey've [the dwarves] brought an apocalypse upon our heads!'", and uses an image that is associated with Armageddon, the end of the world. Peter Jackson. *The Battle of the Five Armies*, 00:00:53-00:00:55.

405 J.R.R. Tolkien, *The Hobbit*, 29.; cf. Peter Jackson. *An Unexpected Journey*, 00:04:38-00:04:40.

406 Cf. Peter Jackson. *An Unexpected Journey*, 00:04:49-00:05:08.

407 The destructive nature of the dragon is hinted at when the dwarves arrive at the Lonely Mountain and see the ruins of the city. The blackened stone hints at Smaug's fiery breath. Cf. Peter Jackson. *The Desolation of Smaug*, 01:28:39.

408 Cf. Corey Olsen. *Exploring* The Hobbit, 255.

409 Cf. Peter Jackson. *An Unexpected Journey*, 00:05:57.

dwarves and the riches buried deep within the mountain.[410] Even though the gate seems to withstand the dragon fire at first, it does not withstand the dragon's (bodily) strength. His strength aids Smaug in destroying most of the objects in the mountain, including those made of stone: apparently solid stone walls suddenly show traces of Smaug's claws as well as cracks and fissures.[411]

Among the halls that have been subject to a reshaping, the treasure chamber is one that shows its transformation most clearly. Smaug, who is attracted by gold and precious objects, wreaks havoc in the treasure chamber when he enters the mountain. Upon entering the chamber the dragon rampages wildly and transforms the formerly neatly-piled hills of gold and artefacts into a sea of gold. This idea is furthered in *The Desolation of Smaug*, in which the dragon is not simply lying on the gold, but is completely covered by it. At the moment when Bilbo enters the enormous chamber and moves some of the pieces of treasure, Smaug's eye is revealed. Sleeping under a blanket of gold, Smaug moves shortly before he wakes up; in this instance, he is reminiscent of a huge sea serpent that surfaces from the water.[412] This example highlights that Smaug has transformed the hall, which can be regarded as one of "the bling-crusted cathedral halls of the mountain"[413], for his own needs, i.e., to satisfy his love of gold by converting the treasure chamber into a bedroom. The reshaping of this hall has apparently also affected the colours of the walls in the mountain, which seem to have lost their symbolic meaning during the dragon's rule. When Bilbo enters the treasure chamber for the first time, the walls appear to be a mixture of sepia, grey and black and to have, just as the gold, become 'pale'.[414] Thus, as in Tolkien's story, architecture and gloom are used to create an eerie atmosphere that is enhanced by the dark or faded colour of the walls. Moreover, Bilbo is afraid of waking the dragon and fears his own echo in the huge hall, as becomes apparent when he politely knocks at the door frame, which produces a hollow echo in the treasure chamber, and immediately goes into hiding.[415] This fear of producing sounds

---

410 Cf. Peter Jackson. *An Unexpected Journey*, 00:05:57.

411 Another significant object made of stone that has been damaged by Smaug is Thror's throne, which represents both the wealth of the former kingdom and its hierarchical structure. When Smaug enters the mountain, the throne (including the bracket for the Arkenstone) and the bridge leading to the throne have been damaged but not destroyed. With the partial destruction of the throne, as the symbol of a king's reign, Jackson indicates that the dwarf kingdom does no longer exist. Cf. Peter Jackson. *The Battle of the Five Armies*, 00:33:13-00:33:18.

412 Similar to Smaug, who hides underneath the masses of gold stored in the mountain, Bilbo can also use a golden object to make himself invisible, namely the ring he has found in Gollum's cave.

413 Kate Muir. "One Film to End Them All.", n.p.

414 Cf. Peter Jackson. *The Desolation of Smaug*, 01:46:15. They do not even regain their original colour when they are illuminated by the dragon's fire. By contrast, the end of *An Unexpected Journey* shows the treasure in its original golden colour, which suggests that this alteration seems to have been made while shooting the second movie.

415 Cf. ibid., 01:45:45-01:45:54.

that might wake the dragon informs Bilbo's exploration of the hoard, as can be seen when he is looking for the Arkenstone in the huge amount of treasure, which causes some noises and echoes.[416] His fear has been fuelled by Balin, who advised the hobbit only briefly beforehand that "'[i]f there is, in fact, a – uhm – live dragon down there, don't waken it'"[417]. Neither of them is sure whether the dragon is still living inside the mountain and they do not doubt that Smaug might be hiding somewhere in the gloom of the enormous halls, which is justified considering that the dragon is completely hidden by gold when Bilbo arrives in the chamber.

The transformation of Erebor by the dragon is also drawn upon by introducing the mountain as a ghost city. This impression is reinforced by using the same setting in two camera shots – before and after the dragon has conquered the mountain. In *An Unexpected Journey*, Bilbo introduces Thror and the camera shows him sitting on his throne, before it pans and shifts into a bird's-eye view revealing the city in the mountain from above. Illuminated by torches, the greenish-blue colour of the walls is set apart by its golden applications and the well-lit paths below indicate that the dwarves are working and mining busily.[418] A similar angle has been adopted for a shot in *The Desolation of Smaug*, where the walls are no longer colourful: the formerly green-coloured walls appear to have become grey and desaturated. The entire scene lacks light, movement and sound, which characterised the shot before, and thus turns the place into a ghost city.[419] By contrast, when the dwarves begin to reshape the mountain in *The Battle of the Five Armies*, the colour symbolism is drawn upon once again. When Fili, Kili, Bofur and Oin enter the mountain, the treasure is shown to be bright golden once again and the walls, illuminated by the treasure, seem to have regained their original colour.[420] With the help of the gold and the mountain's walls, Jackson indicates that the rightful king has returned to Erebor. Thus the colours used when Thorin is shown inside the mountain convey a sense of hope, as they hint at the possibility that Erebor might regain its former glory as a dwarf kingdom.

In the context of Smaug's destruction and the dwarves' exploration of the place, another setting is given special significance, namely the chamber in which the company discovers mummified corpses.[421] Although the chamber does not contain tables or items of feasting as in the original story, it bears some resemblance to Peter Jackson's depiction of Moria in *The Lord of the Rings*, in which

416 Cf. Peter Jackson. *The Desolation of Smaug*, 01:46:47-01:47:53.
417 Ibid., 01:41:24-01:41:34.
418 Cf. Peter Jackson. *An Unexpected Journey*, 00:02:46.
419 Cf. Peter Jackson. *The Desolation of Smaug*, 02:08:17.
420 Cf. Peter Jackson. *The Battle of the Five Armies*, 00:19:20-00:19:49.
421 These corpses are covered in a layer of dust and cobwebs. The facial expressions of the corpses can still be seen and their open eyes and mouths suggest that they suffocated in the small chamber. Cf. Peter Jackson. *The Desolation of Smaug*, 02:11:19.

Boromir concludes, upon seeing a number of corpses, "'[t]his is no mine. It's a tomb'"[422]. In a similar way, Erebor has also been transformed into a tomb for many of its former inhabitants, because, as Thorin notes in *The Hobbit*, "'[n]one escaped that way'"[423]. In the audio-visual adaptation, this idea of being trapped inside the mountain is intensified by depicting men, women and children that died in this chamber. Their corpses highlight an aspect that has been left out of the frame narration in *An Unexpected Journey*, i.e., the fate of those unable to escape Erebor. The discovery of their corpses amplifies the dwarves' feeling of loss that they associate with the place, because they become aware of the agony of their kinsmen, who died, as Thorin puts it, "'[c]owering. Clawing for breath'"[424]. Their death struggle is stressed by the fact that they seem to have attempted to clear the way blocked by stones, which indicates that they suffocated in the chamber. The layer of dust and the cobwebs covering the corpses serve as a reminder of the temporal gap between the attack and the company's return to Erebor. In this respect, the mummification of the corpses does not only remind the company that many years have passed but also that they might even recognise the dwarves in the chamber, because some of their facial features have been preserved.[425] In contrast to the brief reference to "[s]kulls and bones"[426] in *The Hobbit*, the audience is presented with a much more intense imagery of death. Balin's statement that they were "'the last of our kin'"[427] indicates that the dwarves are affected on a deeply personal level. At the same time, the encounter with the corpses of their kinsmen also sparks a sense of retribution in Thorin, who refuses to die like them, and resolutely puts forward that "'[i]f this is to end in fire, then we will all burn together'"[428].

While Smaug destroyed many rooms and halls inside the mountain, 'the Gallery of the Kings' is one of the places that has apparently not yet fallen victim to the dragon's wrath and which is transformed when the dwarves re-enter and reclaim the mountain. In this hall, which has a telling name regarding its function, the temporal gap is important: its dusty banners, which formerly must have added to the royal appearance of the hall, are still hanging on the walls but seem to have faded in colour. The mould set for an enormous dwarf statue is still intact and provides a link between the past and the present. After Thorin and his company have relit the furnaces with the help of Smaug's fiery breath, they fill the mould with liquid gold and complete what their ancestors could not finish

---

422 Peter Jackson. *The Fellowship of the Ring*, 01:41:24-01:41:26.

423 J.R.R. Tolkien. *The Hobbit*, 29.

424 Peter Jackson. *The Desolation of Smaug*, 02:11:40-02:11:44. The dwarves' pity and loss is further enhanced by the soundtrack, which features a slow and melancholic melody produced by string instruments.

425 Cf. ibid., 02:11:13.

426 J.R.R. Tolkien. *The Hobbit*, 279.

427 Peter Jackson. *The Desolation of Smaug*, 02:11:07-02:11:08.

428 Ibid., 02:12:01-02:12:06.

before the dragon attacked.[429] Standing on the mould, Thorin tells Smaug that he is not the King under the Mountain: "'This is not your kingdom. These are Dwarf lands. This is Dwarf gold'"[430] and uses the dwarf-shaped statue to make this unmistakably clear to Smaug. Once the statue has been revealed, Smaug is completely paralysed by its golden appearance and is literally turned into 'Smaug the Golden' when the statue collapses and the gold covers him. Thus, the hall only becomes subject to a transformation when the dwarves have returned and move about in the mountain again.

Given the fact that Peter Jackson's *The Battle of the Five Armies* turns into "a stunning 45-minute CGI battle"[431], the reshaping of the mountain by the dwarves is an aspect that has largely been neglected and has been reduced to the changes made to the front gate. In the movie, the dwarf company fortifies the main entrance with stones; they leave only a small hole, which Thorin uses to speak to Bard.[432] After Bard, unsuccessful in reminding Thorin to keep his word, rode off, the dwarves destroy the bridge that leads into Erebor by levering a head from one of the dwarf statues.[433] In 'decapitating' the dwarf statue, they figuratively also behead their own kingdom. They do not only shut themselves in inside the mountain but simultaneously also prevent anyone from coming close to Erebor. This decision to destroy the bridge expresses their distrust in the other peoples of Middle-earth and highlights that the dwarves (and in particular Thorin) want to keep their treasure for themselves. When the battle starts, the fortification is once more altered and transformed: as soon as Thorin overcomes his avarice and decides that they should join the battle, he and his dwarves use an enormous golden bell to destroy their self-constructed barricade.[434] Given the fact that bells in the adaptations are frequently used to connote danger, the ringing of this bell is used in a different way. There is no danger coming out of the mountain but Thorin and his companions, who are willing to defend Erebor by joining the battle. The bell is thus used as a means to 'open' the front gate again and 'rebuild' the bridge to cross the water. Hence, the destruction of the fortification signifies that Thorin has become aware of the ongoing war and that he and his companions have decided to be part of it.

429 Cf. Peter Jackson. *The Desolation of Smaug*, 02:17:24-02:22:41.

430 Ibid., 02:24:35-02:24:42.

431 Kate Muir. "One Film to End Them All.", n.p.

432 Cf. Peter Jackson. *The Battle of the Five Armies*, 00:43:02-00:44:38.

433 Cf. ibid., 00:45:59-00:46:09.

434 Cf. ibid., 00:18:27; 01:24:09-01:24:24.

Conclusion

In Tolkien's *The Hobbit*, Erebor gains its significance and distinctive meaning from a number of components, as it is not only the destination of the quest but also a place that is subject to transformation more than once. In the beginning, the dwarves reconstruct their former kingdom from their diasporic perspective and remember the ancient dwarf kingdom, its wealth and growth. The dwarf company's collective memories are, however, restricted to their point of view and experiences. Initially, the dwarves are both geographically and temporally distant to the Erebor they once knew. Scattered throughout the country, the dwarves were unable to create a home elsewhere in Middle-earth and still yearn for the mountain. This desire is most clearly expressed in the first part of the 'Song of the Lonely Mountain', in which the dwarves remember their ancestors and the kingdom. It becomes an expression of their longing for and belonging to the mountain and the means to create their 'Erebor of the mind'. This song, which is sung in Bag-End even before the dwarves embark on their journey, implies the dwarves' sense of community on both the content level as well as in the medium of the song. In line with a more general observation by Amy M. Amendt-Raduege, namely that "songs and stories of the past, especially in pre-literate cultures, keep the dead always present, always available, always living"[435], the 'Song of the Lonely Mountain' is used to commemorate the dwarves' ancestors, their treasure and their outstanding skills. The frequent references to the objects they crafted create an emotional connection to the past while simultaneously setting the dwarves of yore apart from other peoples of Middle-earth. Given that the first part of the song is predominantly concerned with memories of the past, they become subject to glorification and idealisation that is closely linked with their diasporic situation at the beginning of the story.

The dwarves' tunnelling and mining inside the mountain is especially relevant in building their kingdom. While the mountain retains its 'natural' looks from the outside, its interior has become subject to transformation. In the protective and enclosed environment of the mountain, the dwarves have not only sung songs and celebrated feasts, but also mined, crafted and stored their golden treasure. Among the huge number of items in their hoard, the most precious one is the Arkenstone of Thrain. The stone is connected with power and greed, which is different to the power connected with the One Ring or the avarice of the dragon, who values quantity over quality. Its special use and function in the former dwarf kingdom manifests itself in its alternative name 'Heart of the Mountain', which bestows animate qualities onto the mountain. Only when the dwarves and the hobbit get gradually closer to the mountain does Bilbo's idea of Erebor, which is based to a great extent on the 'Song of the Lonely Mountain' and Thorin's prose account, transform into a 'lived' place. The closer Bilbo gets

---

435 Amy M. Amendt-Raduege. "'Worthy of a Song': Memory, Mortality and Music.", 115.

to the mountain, the more he is able to confirm or adjust the image he has formed of Erebor before.

In contrast to the glorious depiction of Erebor as an ancient dwarf kingdom, its depiction as a dragon's lair is informed by waste and destruction that manifests in the natural environment surrounding the mountain as well as in Erebor itself. Liam Campbell claims that "Tolkien gave as much detail and passion to the bleak and unwelcoming places of his secondary world creations as he did to the glimmer of his green and vibrant lands"[436], which can, for instance, also be seen in the depiction of the desolation of the dragon. The area surrounding the mountain is shown as a wasteland that is also compared with its former state: the bleak land the dwarves encounter upon their arrival is opposed to the fair land of the old days, and the ruinous city of Dale is compared to its former glory as a prosperous city at the foot of the mountain. These comparisons highlight the transformation of the land and serve the purpose of emphasising the effect the dragon has on the desolate land. The depiction of the dragon's wasteland is also informed by Tolkien's use of Gothic elements, which become manifest in the ruin as a setting, the lack of movements as well as the dangerous and eerie portrayal of the valley in which hardly anything grows. The atmosphere of gloom associated with the area extends to the interior of the mountain: the entrance to the dragon's lair is compared to a 'yawning mouth' that leads into pitch-black darkness. The dragon that lingers at the end of the tunnel enhances this impression. Smaug is introduced as an antagonist as well as a most eerie, dangerous and hybrid creature. His hybridity becomes apparent in his self-description in which he compares himself to natural forces and human weaponry. His ability to speak and his eloquence enhance the danger he poses to the burglar. This mixture of animalistic and human traits adds, according to Midkiff and Jakobsson, to his ambivalent and sinister introduction.[437] Despite the fact that Tolkien used some elements, such as the elaborate entrance into the mountain, which echo dwarvish craft, the eeriness is not resolved. This eeriness is one of the means to create the most striking contrast between the prosperous kingdom of old and the dragon's lair.

Although the transformation of Erebor already begins when the dragon descends and conquers the mountain, the whole scope of this transformation only becomes apparent when the company explores Erebor after the dragon has left and in which the comparisons between the former and the present state prevail. While the halls built by their ancestors initially added to the majestic appearance of the place, they become a dangerous feature when the dragon inhabits the mountain. The tension between past and present is further emphasised in the "'great chamber of Thror'"[438], which contains remnants of human life, i.e.,

[436] Liam Campbell. "Nature.", 434.

[437] Cf. Emily Midkiff. "Uncanny Dragons.", 43.; cf. Ármann Jakobsson. "Talk to the Dragon.", 34.

[438] J.R.R. Tolkien. *The Hobbit*, 279.

bones and skulls, as well as broken artefacts that are subject to decay and covered in a layer of dust. Similarly, the remnants of the bridge also indicate the destruction caused by the fierce marauding of Smaug, who has no use for either the artefacts or the former inhabitants. Both the items associated with feasting and the bridge hint at what the dwarves of old have accomplished and that the interior of the mountain was one of the cultural centres of the dwarves.

The dynamic nature of Erebor as a place is emphasised when the dragon destroys the dwarf kingdom and when Thorin and his company arrive and reshape the mountain. The latter is possible by the spatial proximity of the dwarves to their former kingdom when they arrive at the Lonely Mountain and by the memories and feelings they, and especially Thorin, connect with these halls. The actual transformation of the place is addressed when the dwarves decide to fortify the front gate and block the way with stones. While the dragon has predominantly slept on the treasure, which arguably connects him with passivity, the dwarves' reshaping is something active, which highlights that the dwarves have a use for the chambers and the riches buried inside the mountain. Through their reshaping of the mountain the dwarves create their own place, as the gap between past and present does not permit recreating exactly the place they have lost.

Transformation is also at the core of Peter Jackson's "well-informed yet imaginative reinterpretation"[439] of *The Hobbit*, in which Erebor is created, destroyed and, finally, reshaped. Even though the creation of Erebor and its subsequent destruction are based on the 'Song of the Lonely Mountain' and Thorin's account, the movie adds a further layer of transformation by not only telling but also visually illustrating the events. The narrative voice is given to Bilbo, who tells in a frame narration what happened when the dragon attacked Erebor. In the frame narrative, special emphasis is given to the area surrounding the mountain, including the rich and prosperous city of Dale, which is destroyed during the dragon's attack. After Dale has been turned into a ruin, Smaug attacks the dwarf kingdom, which has been introduced as an impenetrable fortress. The supposed invulnerability associated with the place is reinforced by the huge dwarf statues in front of the mountain, which appear as armoured warriors with levied axes. Apart from being a symbol of warfare and the dwarves' will to defend themselves, they also reflect the dwarves' skill. They are a first hint that the inhabitants have altered the mountain, which is no longer a purely natural place, as can, for instance, be seen with the colour and the shape of the walls. The colours used in the walls hint at the riches that are buried in the depths of the mountain and contribute to Erebor's majestic appearance that has been created by the dwarves.

The dwarves' habitat in the mountain is reminiscent of a city that has been built in its depths. With focus on the spatial arrangement, the position of Thror's

439 Frank P. Riga, Maureen Thum and Judith Kollmann. "From Children's Book to Epic Prequel.", 114.

throne is crucial, as it hints at a hierarchical structure of the dwarf kingdom. On the one hand, a huge stalactite, which is traversed by golden 'veins', protrudes from the ceiling, connects with the throne, and evokes the impression that the gold is flowing directly into the throne of the 'King under the Mountain'. On the other hand, Thror appears to be sitting on all the riches and treasures that can be and have already been found in the vastness of Erebor. The immensity of the place is further emphasised by displaying a hoard that exceeds the expectations of both Bilbo Baggins and the audience. The display of the masses of gold, gemstones and objects also links Thror and the dragon, whose avarice is triggered by the sheer quantity of the treasure.

In Peter Jackson's adaptations the dwarves' kingdom is destroyed when the dragon wrecks the golden-coloured front gate and enters the mountain. The destruction of the front gate is especially striking, because Smaug uses both his fiery breath and his physical strength to destroy the gate, which is, due to its decorations, an emblem of the dwarves' culture. Both the front gate and Thror's throne are charged with meaning, because both are associated with the success and wealth of the dwarf kingdom, especially since they are ornamented with dwarvish symbols and runes. In the context of Smaug's attack, both get destroyed: the front gate is smashed into pieces and the throne is demolished, which highlights that the dragon is about to transform the place into his lair.

In Peter Jackson's *The Desolation of Smaug*, Thorin and his company manage to enter the mountain again and realise that it has changed visibly. The spacious but dark halls of Erebor are associated with gloom and danger and the transformation from a splendid city into a ghost town and tomb takes its full effect in the movie. The gap between past and present is, for example, highlighted in the chamber that contains mummified bodies of dwarves. This chamber is not only reminiscent of Jackson's depiction of Moria in *The Lord of the Rings*, but also of the 'chamber of Thror' in *The Hobbit*. Instead of showing only bones and skulls, Jackson apparently opted for creating a sentimental layer by depicting a mass grave of dwarves, who were trapped inside the mountain and suffocated in the small room and whose facial features can still be recognised. With depictions like this, Jackson has not only transformed the text into the medium of film but also enhanced the feeling of loss.

Similar to his actions in the novel, Thorin also starts to fortify the main entrance in Jackson's adaptation and reshapes the mountain in *The Battle of the Five Armies*. As soon as the dwarves enter the mountain, Thorin is deeply affected by dragon-sickness and bases his decisions on his avarice. Among these is his command to barricade the front gate so that no one can enter the mountain. The dwarves, however, do not only block the front gate successfully, they also destroy the bridge that leads towards the gate by levering the head of a dwarf statue from the statue's shoulders; this way they hope to ensure that no other will claim the mountain. Apart from building a fortification to prevent others from entering Erebor, the dwarves later change the front gate once more: they use the bell that was brought down when the dragon entered the mountain to eventually destroy the fortification. Apart from a dwarf-made transformation, the walls seem to react to the presence of Thorin and his companions on their own accord. During the dragon's rule in *The Desolation of Smaug* the walls were sepia-grey coloured, but they regain their greenish colour once the dragon has left and has been killed, which is a transformation that permits the assumption that the rightful king has returned.

Works Cited

Abbott, H. Porter. *The Cambridge Introduction to Narrative*. Second Edition. Cambridge: Cambridge University Press, 2008 [2002].

Acker, Paul, Matthew Bardowell, and Jeffrey A. Weinstock. "Dwarf." *The Ashgate Encyclopedia of Literary and Cinematic Monsters*. Ed. Jeffrey A. Weinstock. Farnham and Burlington (Vermont): Ashgate, 2014. 197-201.

Amendt-Raduege, Amy M. "'Worthy of a Song': Memory, Mortality and Music." *Middle-earth Minstrel – Essays on Music in Tolkien.* Ed. Bradford Lee Eden. Jefferson (North Carolina) and London: McFarland, 2010. 114-125.

Anderson, Douglas A. (Ed.). *Das große Hobbit Buch.* J.R.R. Tolkien. Trans. Wolfgang Krege and Lisa Kuppler. Stuttgart: Klett-Cotta, 2012.

Apseloff, Marilyn, and Alethea Helbig. "Place in Children's Literature." *Children's Literature Association Quarterly* 8.1 (1983): 9.

Ashcroft, Bill, Gareth Griffiths, and Helen Tiffin. *Post-Colonial Studies: The Key Concepts*. Abingdon and New York: Routledge-Taylor & Francis, 2006 [1998].

---. "Diaspora." *The Post-Colonial Studies Reader*. Eds. Bill Ashcroft, Gareth Griffiths, and Helen Tiffin. Second Edition. Abingdon and New York: Routledge-Taylor & Francis, 2007 [1995]. 425-427.

Atherton, Mark. *There and Back Again – J R R Tolkien and the Origins of The Hobbit.* London and New York: I.B. Tauris, 2012.

Baum, L. Frank. *The Wonderful Wizard of Oz*. *The Annotated Wizard of Oz*. Ed. Michael Patrick Hearn. Centennial Edition. New York: W.W. Norton, 2000 [1900].

Boym, Svetlana. *The Future of Nostalgia*. New York: Basic Books, 2001.

Brah, Avtar. "Thinking Through the Concept of Diaspora." *The Post-Colonial Studies Reader*. Eds. Bill Ashcroft, Gareth Griffiths, and Helen Tiffin. Second Edition. Abingdon and New York: Routledge-Taylor & Francis, 2007 [1995]. 443-446.

Buchholz, Sabine, and Manfred Jahn. "Space in Narrative." *Routledge Encyclopedia of Narrative Theory*. Eds. David Herman, Manfred Jahn, and Marie-Laure Ryan. Abingdon and New York: Routledge-Taylor & Francis, 2005. 551-555.

Campbell, Liam. "Nature." *A Companion to J.R.R. Tolkien.* Ed. Stuart D. Lee. Malden (Massachusetts), Oxford and Chichester: John Wiley & Sons, 2014. 431-445.

Carpenter, Humphrey (Ed.). *Letters of J.R.R. Tolkien – A Selection Edited by Humphrey Carpenter with the Assistance of Christopher Tolkien*. London: George Allen and Unwin, 1981.

Carroll, Jane Suzanne. *Landscape in Children's Literature*. New York and Abingdon: Routledge-Taylor & Francis, 2011.

---. "A Topoanalytical Reading of Landscapes in *The Lord of the Rings* and *The Hobbit*." *J.R.R. Tolkien –* The Hobbit *and* The Lord of the Rings. Ed. Peter Hunt. Basingstoke and New York: Palgrave Macmillan, 2013. 121-138.

Chance, Jane. *Tolkien's Art – A Mythology for England*. Revised Edition. Lexington (Kentucky): The University Press of Kentucky, 2001.

Chrostowska, S.D. "Consumed by Nostalgia?" *SubStance* 39.2 (2010): 52-70.

Clifford, James. "Diasporas." *The Post-Colonial Studies Reader*. Eds. Bill Ashcroft, Gareth Griffiths, and Helen Tiffin. Second Edition. Abingdon and New York: Routledge-Taylor & Francis, 2007 [1995]. 451-454.

Cohen, Jeffrey Jerome. "Monster Culture (Seven Theses)." *Monster Theory – Reading Culture*. Ed. Jeffrey Jerome Cohen. Minneapolis (Minnesota): University of Minnesota Press, 1996. 3-25.

Cresswell, T. "Place." *International Encyclopedia of Human Geography*. Eds. Rob Kitchin and Nigel Thrift. Amsterdam et al.: Elsevier, 2009. 169-177.

Davis, Fred. "Nostalgia, Identity and the Current Nostalgia Wave." *Journal of Popular Culture* 11.2 (1977): 414-424.

Dickinson, Greg, Carole Blair, and Brian L. Ott. "Introduction: Rhetoric/Memory/Place." *Places of Public Memory: The Rhetoric of Museums and Memorials*. Eds. Greg Dickinson, Carole Blair, and Brian L. Ott. Tuscaloosa (Alabama): The University of Alabama Press 2010. 1-54.

Döring, Tobias. *Postcolonial Literatures in English*. Stuttgart: Klett, 2008.

Eden, Bradford Lee. "Introduction." The Hobbit *and Tolkien's Mythology – Essays on Revisions and Influences*. Ed. Bradford Lee Eden. Jefferson (North Carolina): McFarland, 2014. 1-4.

Edwards, Justin. D. *Postcolonial Literature*. Basingstoke and New York: Palgrave Macmillan, 2008.

Eigler, Friederike. *Heimat, Space, Narrative – Toward a Transnational Approach to Flight and Expulsion*. Woodbridge and Rochester (New York): Camden House-Boydell & Brewer, 2014.

Foster, Robert. *A Guide to Middle-Earth*. New York and Toronto (Canada): Ballantine Books, 1977 [1971].

Foucault, Michel. "Of Other Spaces." Trans. Jay Miskowiec. *Diacritics* 16.1 (1986): 22-27.

Gullón, Ricardo. "On Space in the Novel." *Critical Inquiry* 2.1 (1975): 11-28.

Hallet, Wolfgang, and Birgit Neumann. "Raum und Bewegung in der Literatur: Zur Einführung." *Raum und Bewegung in der Literatur: Die Literaturwissenschaft und der Spatial Turn*. Eds. Wolfgang Hallet and Birgit Neumann. Bielefeld: Transcript, 2009. 11-32.

Hynes, Gerard. "From Nauglath to Durin's Folk – *The Hobbit* and Tolkien's Dwarves." The Hobbit *and Tolkien's Mythology – Essays on Revisions and Influences*. Ed. Bradford Lee Eden. Jefferson (North Carolina): McFarland, 2014. 20-37.

Jackson, Peter (Dir.). *The Hobbit – An Unexpected Journey*. Warner Bros., Metro-Goldwyn-Mayer and New Line Cinema, 2012.

---. *The Hobbit – The Battle of the Five Armies*, Warner Bros., Metro-Goldwyn-Mayer and New Line Cinema, 2014.

---. *The Hobbit – The Desolation of Smaug*. Warner Bros., Metro-Goldwyn-Mayer and New Line Cinema, 2013.

---. *The Lord of the Rings – The Fellowship of the Ring*. Warner Bros. and New Line Cinema, 2002.

Jakobsson, Ármann. "Talk to the Dragon: Tolkien as Translator." *Tolkien Studies* 6 (2009): 27-39.

Jeremiah, Milford A. "The Use of Place in Writing and Literature." *Language Arts Journal of Michigan* 16.2 (2000): 23-27.

Kaveney, Roz. "Dragons." *The Encyclopedia of Fantasy*. Eds. John Clute and John Grant. London: Orbit, 1997. 295-296.

Keats, John. "La Belle Dame Sans Merci." *John Keats – Selected Poetry*. Ed. Elizabeth Cook. Oxford and New York: Oxford University Press, 1998 [1994]. 166-167.

Leeming, David. *The Oxford Companion to World Mythology*. New York: Oxford University Press, 2005.

Lewis, C.S. *The Voyage of the Dawn Treader*. New York: HarperCollins, 2002 [1952].

Liddell, Henry George, and Robert Scott. *A Greek-English Lexicon*. Oxford: Clarendon Press, 1901.

Lüthi, Max. *The Fairytale – As Art Form and Portrait of Man*. Trans. Jon Erickson. Bloomington (Indiana): Indiana University Press, 1987 [1975].

Malpas, J.E. *Place and Experience – A Philosophical Topography*. Cambridge: Cambridge University Press, 1999.

Manlove, Colin. *The Fantasy Literature of England*. Basingstoke and New York: Macmillan and St. Martin's Press, 1999.

McLeod, John. *Beginning Postcolonialism*. Second Edition. Manchester and New York: Manchester University Press, 2010 [2000].

Midkiff, Emily. "'Dragons are Tricksy': The Uncanny Dragons of Children's Literature." *Fafnir – Nordic Journal of Science Fiction and Fantasy Research* 1.2 (2014): 41-54. Last access: 20 October 2017. <http://journal.finfar.org/articles/76.pdf>

Muir, Kate. "One Film to End Them All; the Big Movie Peter Jackson's Farewell to Hobbits and Middle-earth is All Killer Battle Scenes and no Filler." *The Times*. 12. Dec. 2014. Last access: 17 October 2017. <http://www.lexisnexis.com/lnacui2api/api/version1/getDocCui?lni=5DTK-XPK1-JBVM-Y3WF&csi=10939&hl=t&hv=t&hnsd=f&hns=t&hgn=t&oc=00240&perma=true>

Nodelman, Perry, and Mavis Reimer. *The Pleasures of Children's Literature*. Third Edition. Boston (Massachusetts): Allyn and Bacon-Pearson Education, 2003 [1992].

Olsen, Corey. *Exploring J.R.R. Tolkien's* The Hobbit. Boston and New York: Houghton Mifflin Harcourt, 2012.

Pavlik, Anthony. *A View from Elsewhere: The Spatiality of Children's Fantasy Fiction*. Diss. Newcastle University, 2011. Last access: 20 October 2017. <https://theses.ncl.ac.uk/dspace/bitstream/10443/1891/1/Pavlik11.pdf>

Rateliff, John D. *The History of The Hobbit – One-Volume Edition*. London: HarperCollins, 2013 [2007].

---. "Anchoring the Myth – The Impact of *The Hobbit* on Tolkien's Legendarium." The Hobbit *and Tolkien's Mythology – Essays on Revisions and Influences*. Ed. Bradford Lee Eden. Jefferson (North Carolina): McFarland, 2014. 6-19.

Rauer, Christine. *Beowulf and the Dragon – Parallels and Analogues*. Diss. Woodbridge and Rochester (New York): D.S. Brewer-Boydell & Brewer, 2000.

Riga, Frank P., Maureen Thum, and Judith Kollmann. "From Children's Book to Epic Prequel: Peter Jackson's Transformation of Tolkien's *The Hobbit*." *Mythlore* 32.2 (2014): 97-115.

Rowling, J.K. *Harry Potter and the Philosopher's Stone*. London: Bloomsbury, 1997.

Rushdie, Salman. "Imaginary Homelands." *Imaginary Homelands – Essays and Criticism 1981-1991*. Salman Rushdie. London: Granta Books/Penguin, 1991. 9-21.

Schröder, Nicole. *Spaces and Places in Motion – Spatial Concepts in Contemporary American Literature*. Diss. Tübingen: Gunter Narr, 2006.

Shippey, Tom. *The Road to Middle-earth*. Revised and Expanded Edition. London: HarperCollins, 2005 [1982].

Sibley, Brian. *The Hobbit: The Desolation of Smaug – Official Movie Guide*. Boston and New York: Houghton Mifflin Harcourt, 2013.

Simek, Rudolf. *Mittelerde – Tolkien und die germanische Mythologie*. München: C.H. Beck, 2005.

Smith, Andrew. *Gothic Literature*. Edinburgh: Edinburgh University Press, 2008 [2007].

Snodgrass, Mary Ellen. *Encyclopedia of Gothic Literature*. New York: Facts on File, 2005.

Stanton, Michael N. *Hobbits, Elves, and Wizards – Exploring the Wonders and Worlds of J.R.R. Tolkien's* The Lord of the Rings. New York and Basingstoke: Palgrave Macmillan, 2002 [2001].

Tolkien, J.R.R. "Beowulf: The Monsters and the Critics." *DISCovering Authors*. Online ed. Detroit: Gale, 2003. Discovering Collection. Gale. Gwinnett County Public Schools. Last access: 14 May 2008. <http://find.galegroup.com/srcx/infomark.do?&contentSet=GSRC&type=retrieve&tabID=T001&prodId=DC&docId=EJ2101201744&source=gale&srcprod=DISC&userGroupName=lawr16325&version=1.0>

---. "Farmer Giles of Ham." *Tales from the Perilous Realm*. J.R.R. Tolkien. London: HarperCollins, 2008 [1949]. 99-165.

---. *The Hobbit, or There and Back Again*. London: HarperCollins, 2006 [1937].

---. *The Lord of the Rings – The Fellowship of the Ring*. London: HarperCollins, 2007 [1954].

---. *The Lord of the Rings – The Return of the King*. London: HarperCollins, 2007 [1955].

---. "The Quest of Erebor." *Unfinished Tales of Númenor and Middle-earth*. J.R.R. Tolkien. Ed. Christopher Tolkien. London: HarperCollins, 2014 [1980]. 415-435.

---. *The Silmarillion*. Ed. Christopher Tolkien. London: HarperCollins, 1999 [1977].

---. "Tree and Leaf." *The Tolkien Reader*. J.R.R. Tolkien. New York: Del Rey-Random House, 1966. 29-120.

Tyler, J.E.A. *The Tolkien Companion*. New York: Gramercy Books-Random House, 2000 [1976].

Unerman, Sandra. “Dragons in Twentieth-Century Fiction.” *Folklore* 113.1 (2002): 94-101.

Vink, Renée. “‘Jewish’ Dwarves: Tolkien and Anti-Semitic Stereotyping.” *Tolkien Studies* 10 (2013): 123-145.

Waddey, Lucy. “Home in Children’s Fiction: Three Patterns.” *Children’s Literature Association Quarterly* 8.1 (1983): 13-15.

Walder, Dennis. *Postcolonial Nostalgias – Writing, Representation, and Memory*. Abingdon and New York: Routledge-Taylor & Francis, 2011.

Walker, Steve. *The Power of Tolkien’s Prose – Middle-Earth’s Magical Style*. Basingstoke and New York: Palgrave Macmillan, 2009.

Wilson, Melissa B., and Kathy G. Short. “Goodbye Yellow Brick Road: Challenging the Mythology of Home in Children’s Literature.” *Children’s Literature in Education* 43 (2012): 129-144.

Zoran, Gabriel. “Towards a Theory of Space in Narrative.” *Poetics Today* 5.2 (1984): 309-335.

Appendix: 'Song of the Lonely Mountain'[440]

Far over the misty mountains cold
To dungeons deep and caverns old
We must away ere break of day
To seek the pale enchanted gold.

The dwarves of yore made mighty spells,
While hammers fell like ringing bells
In places deep, where dark things sleep,
In hollow halls beneath the fells.

For ancient king and elvish lord
There many a gleaming golden hoard
They shaped and wrought, and light they caught
To hide in gems on hilt of sword.

On silver necklaces they strung
The flowering stars, on crowns they hung
The dragon-fire, in twisted wire
They meshed the light of moon and sun.

Far over the misty mountains cold
To dungeons deep and caverns old
We must away, ere break of day,
To claim our long-forgotten gold.

Goblets they carved there for themselves
And harps of gold; where no man delves
There lay they long, and many a song
Was sung unheard by men or elves.

[440] J.R.R. Tolkien. *The Hobbit*, 18-19, original emphasis.

The pines were roaring on the height,
The winds were moaning in the night.
The fire was red, it flaming spread;
The trees like torches blazed with light.

The bells were ringing in the dale
And men looked up with faces pale;
The dragon's ire more fierce than fire
Laid low their towers and houses frail.

The mountain smoked beneath the moon;
The dwarves, they heard the tramp of doom.
They fled their hall to dying fall
Beneath his feet, beneath the moon.

Far over the misty mountains grim
To dungeons deep and caverns dim
We must away, ere break of day,
To win our harps and gold from him!

Zeitfracht Medien GmbH
Ferdinand-Jühlke-Straße 7
99095 Erfurt, Deutschland
produktsicherheit@kolibri360.de